Mind Chatter
That Matters

Mind Chatter That Matters

The Ultimate Guide to your Inner Conflict

by Liz Atherton

CONSCIOUS CARE PUBLISHING PTY LTD

Mind Chatter That Matters
The Ultimate Guide to Your Inner Conflict

Copyright © 2014 by Liz Atherton. All rights reserved.

First Published 2015 by: Conscious Care Publishing Pty Ltd
www.consciouscarepublishing.com

Second Edition printed December 2016.

Notice of Rights
This book is sold subject to the condition that it shall not, by way of trade or otherwise, be lent, resold, hired out, or otherwise circulated without the publisher's prior consent, in any form of binding or cover, other than that in which it is published, and without a similar condition, including this condition being imposed on the subsequent purchaser. All rights reserved by the publisher. No part of this publication may be reproduced, stored in a retrieval system, or transmitted in any form, or by any means, electronic, digital, mechanical, photocopying, scanning, recorded or otherwise, without the prior written permission of the copyright owner. Requests to the copyright owner should be addressed to Permissions Department, Conscious Care Publishing Pty Ltd, email admin@consciouscare.com

Categories
1. Self Help. 2. New Age. 3. Wellbeing. 4. Mind 5. Mind, Body, Spirit

Limits of Liability/Disclaimer of Warranty:
While the publisher and author have used their best efforts in preparing this book, they make no representations or warranties with respect to the accuracy or completeness of the contents of this book and specifically disclaim any implied warranties of merchantability or fitness for a particular purpose. No warranty may be created or extended by sales representatives or written sales materials. The author of this book does not dispense medical advice or prescribe the use of any technique as a form of treatment for physical, emotional, or medical problems without the advice of a physician, either directly or indirectly. The advice and strategies contained herein may not be suitable for your situation. You should consult with a professional where appropriate. The intent of the author is only to offer information for a general nature to help you in your request for a happier life. Neither the publisher nor author shall be liable for any loss of profit or any other commercial damages, including but not limited to special, incidental, consequential, or other damages. The author and the publisher assume no responsibility for your actions.

Conscious Care Publishing publishes in a variety of print and electronic format and by print-on-demand. Some material included with standard print versions of this book may not be included in e-books or in print-on-demand. If this book refers to media such as a CD or DVD that is not included in the version you purchased, you may download this material at https://consciouscarepublishing.com

National Library of Australia Cataloguing-in-Publication entry:
Author: Atherton, Liz, 1963-
Mind Chatter That Matters : The Ultimate Guide to Your Inner Conflict / by Liz Atherton
ISBN 9780994540485 (Paperback), 9780994540492 (Digital)
Atherton, Liz, 1963-

Banot, Marvel, Cover Illustrator.
Elvira Mikhralieva, Interior Illustrator
Rocky Hudson, Editor
158.1
Printed by Lightning Source
Typeset by Conscious Care Publishing Pty Ltd
ISBN: 978-0-9945404-8-5

To my miracles,

Katie and Lachlan.

I love you eternally.

CONTENTS

Introduction
Why you need to Read this Book — 1
The Physical Brain — 5
    Our fight/flight/freeze reflex — 7
    Right-brained vs. Left-brained — 8
    The Male vs. Female brain — 9
The Mind's Roles — 11
    The three parts of the mind — 13
    The Three Psychic Apparatuses — 15
    A new understanding - Analytical Psychology — 24
Unpacking the Confusion — 29
    Emotions and their role — 31
    The inadequate and inferior mask — 44
    Anxiety — 47
    Depression — 47
    You are more than your thoughts and emotions — 52
Your Beliefs & Values — 57
    Who's to blame? — 63
Your Blocks — 67
    Accountability and responsibility — 68
    Blind Spots in your Awareness — 69
    Looking outside for your answers — 72
    Up until now who has been your decision maker? — 74
Digging up your Trash & Treasure — 81
    Do not be fooled by your Parent's clever guise — 87

Reprogramming your storage	89
How we beat ourselves up during Inner Conflict	94
Fears – real or imagined?	95
Uncomfortable comfort zones	95
Your Intuitive Self	**97**
Your Intuitive Self's purpose	101
How the Intuitive Self communicates to you	104
Becoming open to your Intuitive Self	106
Trusting your Intuitive Self voice	110
You are a creative being	111
Choosing the voice that wins	113
How can you integrate?	115
Light vs. Dark	118
True goal setting	119
Mind – body relationship	119
When your Intuitive Self voice is awakening, speaking and guiding you	121
Self-care	**131**
Steps for Self-care	132
Practice changes for the next 30 days	146
References	**151**
Further Information	**153**
Authors Note	**155**
Acknowledgements	**159**

INTRODUCTION

This book is about finding personal freedom, happiness, your true purpose, and the passion to live the life you have always dreamed of.

All of us have limitations or feel trapped in some way, whether it is anger, depression, grief, anxiety, or an overwhelming sense of failure and disillusionment because life is not what we expected it to be. No matter how many times you want to change, or try to become whole, free, and joyful, your attempts may appear fruitless.

When you learn how your mind works, what other resources you can use to overcome the endless mind chatter you experience, you can gain control over your thoughts and decisions to bring real happiness and joy into your life.

Nothing in your life is written in stone: regardless of how bleak it has been, or appears to be, you have the power to change it. This book is designed to help you overcome a lifetime of negative unconscious information which you have stored in your mind, and hinders you from attaining the freedom of your own self-expression and existence.

I hope this book brings more clarity to your inner voices. It will help you to know and trust your own Intuitive Self, your inner guidance system, which shall never let you down, ever!

Love and blessings,

Liz x

- Chapter 1 -

WHY YOU NEED TO READ THIS BOOK

To become the master of your inner conflict you first need to understand how your mind works, and to do this you need to understand the abilities of your brain and mind.

This book may challenge you as it will stretch your thinking, which is exactly what it is meant to do. Reading its entire content is important to enable you to grasp the methods of learning about your inner voices together with each of their agendas and how they sound within you. Opting out without completing it will be your egos way of controlling your thoughts to enable its survival, rather than allow you to become more centred and able to operate from your true

Mind Chatter That Matters

inner self. The ego mind has a fantastic method of concealing its own agenda from your awareness, and is very self-sabotaging, so I challenge you to read this book through to completion so that you will have the knowledge to become a master of your own thoughts and the direction your life will take.

Your ego is a part of your human mind often referred to as your "will" or "devil". This part of your mind can be the most damaging, self-defeating and controlling influence over your thoughts, decisions and life direction. It will fight for its own survival, as if it doesn't run your life's thoughts and decisions, it feels like life will end and death will result. It will drastically sabotage your efforts to prevent anything else from running your mind, including your gut instincts! Comprehending this agenda of your ego mind is crucial in becoming a master of your own thoughts and the decisions you make in the future.

To enable you to understand how your ego mind operates, you need to first learn about the parts of your ego mind and what purpose each holds. In addition to that I will introduce a further voice, which is that of the soul. This voice of the soul can be called many things, including gut instinct, higher self, inner self, intuitive self. Within this book I call your soul's voice your "Intuitive Self".

In order to conquer the ego mind and its desperate need to dominate your decisions, regardless of how self-sabotaging those decisions may be, you need to understand the inner conflict between the ego mind's voices and comprehend how to observe your thoughts; you then must learn how to listen to your Intuitive Self. This is the voice that truly matters as it will guide you through every difficult life

Why you need to Read this Book

situation, important decision and temporary loss of direction. It will work with you to guide you to a path of happiness and purpose in your life.

Throughout my career I have specialised in helping thousands of people discern their gut instinct or Intuitive Self and how it operates within them. During consultations I help clients establish the meaning of the Intuitive Self's messages and teach them how to act on them even when there is inner conflict within the ego mind.

I have witnessed clients grow enormously, escaping from depression, anxiety and fears to feel fulfilled and whole, and, for the first time, in control of their lives. Once you understand the voices within your mind, you gain control whilst you are experiencing inner turmoil; whilst you are still feeling stuck and unclear of how to move through the problems in your life. So I challenge you to complete this book and not allow your ego mind to prevent you from finishing it!

My joy and pleasure in life is in helping others gain happiness and fulfillment through my work. I know that reading this book can be challenging for your comprehension. It may suit you more to do this kind of personal development in a face to face scenario, to enrol in one of my online courses in Mind Chatter, to watch my webinars or to attend one of my retreats. These are all ways I can help you discern your inner voice from your ego's voice and learn what your soul is trying to instruct you to do.

My work feels like pleasure because I'm doing what I was born to do and I am therefore in my element of purpose and passion. I want the same for you. For your life to be happy and whole. I totally embrace

Mind Chatter That Matters

being a guiding light to many and will continue to help bring the people of this world into a better place; emotionally, mentally and physically. I welcome you to your inner journey of discovering your true self, your past beliefs and patterns that now longer serve you, and the changes you have the power to make every day! We have all made silly decisions that didn't help us, or made our life take a turn for the worse. Beating yourself up about the past will not help your future and it is the ego mind's way of blocking growth and happiness within you.

You will discover in next two chapters how your physical mind works, along with the history and understanding of the psychological human mind. This information may be a little boring or bland, but please don't skip these two chapters as they are imperative to your learning. Although they are a little technical, they are important because I refer back to them throughout the book. Each chapter is essential to your learning.

So come on board, push through this book, regardless of your resistance to completing it. You know you want happiness and contentment in your life. It is just a few pages away!

Feel free to join me on my website at www.lizatherton.com where you will find further inspiration for your life journey.

- CHAPTER 2 -

THE PHYSICAL BRAIN

This chapter will begin with a little anatomy lesson. You will then learn how your conflict starts and goes on and on and on.

Every human has a brain and your body cannot function without one! The brain is a fascinating organ which designates instructions to our bodies at an outstanding rate. The central nervous system (which consists of the brain and the spinal cord) operates like an internal universe. All components need to be in balance, and externally sourced nutrition is necessary for the system to survive and operate at an optimum level. The brain's ability to instruct the body to breathe, heal and keep the heart beating is something that we do not fully understand, yet take for granted each and every day of our lives.

Scientists have made statements and presented factual information for centuries, but the truth is, no one really knows how much of the mind we use. Although every neuron in the brain is continually active, even if firing very slowly, many people believe that we only use a small percentage of our brains. This belief came about because when electroencephalograms began to be used they could detect only a small percentage of the brain's activity. Is it true that we only use a very small of our brain's potential, or is this a myth that has been perpetuated due to the limited ability of humans to measure what the brain is doing? How is it that someone who is brain damaged can have another portion of their brain take over the role of the damaged portion? Why is it that the brain can sometimes be damaged beyond repair? For many years scientists claimed that, unlike other organs in our body, the brain could not regenerate cells to heal and repair. However, more recent studies have proved the brain is capable of cellular genesis.

We do not fully understand the brain and how it works and have a limited understanding of the mind's potential and its role in our lives, and I don't believe we can even begin to conceptualise what it is capable of. Each time the scientists believe they have got it right another concept is revealed.

Our fight/flight/freeze reflex

All beings in the animal kingdom, including humans, have been

The Physical Brain

gifted with an autonomic nervous system that acts unconsciously and regulates daily bodily functions such as heart rate, digestion, papillary response, urination and sexual arousal. This system is the primary mechanism in the control of the fight, flight or freeze response and its role is mediated by two different components—the sympathetic and parasympathetic nervous systems.

The sympathetic nervous system originates in the spinal cord. It is responsible for the release of norepinephrine or noradrenalin, which activates the physiological changes that occur during the flight or fight response. This response is triggered by real or imagined threats and takes effect in as little as a twentieth of a second. It tells your heart to beat faster, tells the muscles to tense and prepare so you can fight harder and run faster, tells the eyes to dilate to see better and tells the mucous membranes to dry so you can breathe better.

The parasympathetic nervous system originates in the spinal cord and medulla and typically functions in opposition to the sympathetic nervous system but is complementary in nature rather than antagonistic. The parasympathetic nervous system releases the neurotransmitter acetylcholine to activate the relaxation response. It tells the body, "It is okay, you can relax now, the danger has passed, and there is no need to be on alert anymore." The same chemical is released to allow us to sleep when we turn the lights out at night. These same neurotransmitters, hormones and pain killers that help the body relax are also dumped into the bloodstream in huge amounts when the freeze response kicks in. This is how the mortally wounded can lie still.

Only recently has the freeze reflex been recognised as an additional instinctual response. This freeze reflex is activated when a person or animal is frozen in fear and often stares at the source of danger. Or, in another example, an animal in the woods may survive better by freezing or "acting dead" when encountering another animal hunting for prey by movement.

These fight, flight and freeze reflexes are part of our basic human survival instinct and cannot be overridden by our thoughts. However our thoughts can still assess the situation and make a decision on how to handle it.

Right-brained vs. Left-brained

Have you ever heard people refer to others as being more right-brained or left-brained? Perhaps you have read books or watched television programs that refer to these terms. It might surprise you to learn that although people have different styles of thinking, it is simply a myth that we use one side of our brains or the other.

The term "right-brained" or "left-brained" comes from a psychological theory known as lateralization of brain function. Right-brained people are often said to be more intuitive, creative, thoughtful and subjective. Left-brained people are said to be more logical, analytical and objective.

It is now known that one side of the brain does not dominate the other, with both hemispheres working simultaneously and communicating through the corpus callosum.

The Physical Brain

The Male vs. Female brain

Well, scientists have proven that the male brain is indeed approximately 6.5 percent bigger than the female brain, but this does not take into account the fact that men are normally of greater stature. Before those male heads start to swell, we need to consider that female brains have 10 times more white matter than those of males. The different ratios of white and grey matter may be the reason men and women think and process their thoughts so differently.

In 2001, researchers from Harvard found that certain parts of the male and female brain that were used for the same function were different in size, which evens out the overall difference. The increased size of the male brain must be balanced against the increased proportion of the females' white matter. Grey matter is full of active neurons while the less dense white matter has more connections between the neurons, resulting in a faster working result. Men tend to think with grey matter, women with white. Therefore in women neurons are less densely packed, but the extensive connections between neurons makes thinking quicker. The density of these neurons has not been shown to be correlated with intelligence.

Studies carried out at the University of Pennsylvania in the US now provide further material for the nature versus nurture debate. The female brain has been found to be wired differently to the male brain. Female brains have stronger left-to-right circuits with links between reasoning and intuition, while male brains tend to have stronger front-to-back circuits with links between perception and action. The brain's so-called connectome matched observed behavioural differences between the sexes. Women did better at tests of attention, word and face memory and cognition. Men did better on spatial processing, motor skills and sensorimotor speed.

Nevertheless, we must remember there are subtle differences to the social conditioning of boys and girls, born as they are into a world where it's impressed on their little brains that pink is for girls and blue for boys. Some people say these factors are difficult to ignore when considering the human brain at birth.

And as for intelligence, average IQ scores for men and women are the same.

What do we deem to be intelligence anyway? Is it the ability to think quickly, is it academic ability? Is emotional intelligence not equally as important? The truth is that intelligence is a balancing act. People are gifted differently depending on their individual life purposes. We all have a unique intellectual predisposition and a unique life experience, and these factors impact on what we store into our unconscious and preconscious minds.

- Chapter 3 -

THE MIND'S ROLE

The origin of the modern concept of consciousness is usually attributed to John Locke's Essay *Concerning Human Understanding*, published in 1690 [1]. Locke defined consciousness as "the perception of what passes in a man's own mind"[2].

As far back as the 18th Century the term "unconscious mind" was coined by philosopher Friedrich Schelling. However it was the Austrian-born neurologist and psychoanalyst Sigmund Freud (6 May 1856 – 23 September 1939) who became known as the founding father of psychoanalysis. Sigmund Freud and his followers developed a topographical division of the psyche into the conscious

Mind Chatter That Matters

and unconscious mind. Freud coined further terms for distinct areas of the mind: the conscious mind, the preconscious mind and the unconscious mind, together with the ID, Ego and Super-Ego, which relate to the unconscious and its defences.

Freud also believed that dreams and other significant psychic events that take place "below the surface" in the unconscious mind allow us to see our unconscious urges and needs in order to fulfil these needs. He interpreted these psychic events as having both symbolic and actual significance.

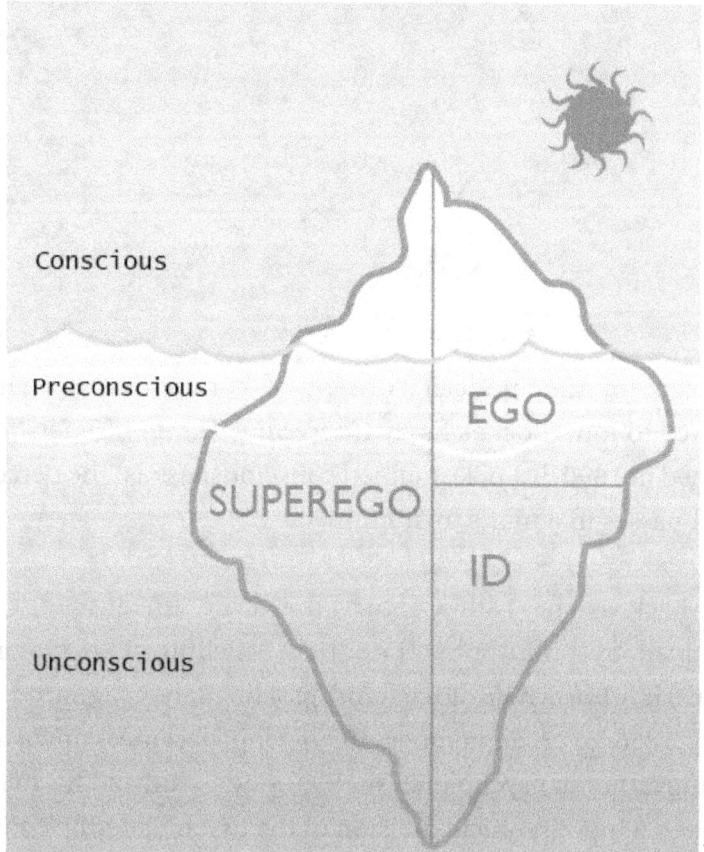

Figure 1

The Mind's Role

The three parts of the mind

The Conscious Mind

The conscious mind is also termed "consciousness" or "mindfulness". Despite the difficulty in defining it, many philosophers believe that it is the quality or state of being aware of something internal or external.

The conscious mind is the executive control system, the observer, the decision maker and the strategist. It allows you to become aware of your mental and bodily functions as well as external occurrences happening to and around you.

Being internally aware is to have an awareness of one's thoughts, feelings, experiences, wakefulness and sense of self.

Being externally aware is to have an awareness of what is happening to you or around you.

We often live in what I deem to be "automatic pilot" state. How often have you gone for a walk or driven a car and not even realised that you have travelled where you have? Your conscious mind was not on the task at hand, not aware of your "doing", but somewhere else thinking about something else.

So where was your mind? External or internal factors can trigger your thinking, and your consciousness can wander away from your experience. So, depending on your thoughts, you can lose consciousness and become machine-like in your thinking and actions. This is where we begin to operate from the preconscious or unconscious mind.

Later in the book you will discover how your conscious mind is your most powerful tool in observing Mind Chatter. It can direct decisions to override the decisions of other parts of your preconscious mind and unconscious mind.

According to Freud, there are two distinctive types of unconscious mind – in one type thoughts are easily brought into the conscious or preconscious, while in the other type thoughts are difficult if not impossible to bring into consciousness.

The Preconscious Mind

The preconscious mind is where we store information and thoughts that are not repressed and are easily available for recall into our conscious mind for cognitive processing. In other words, everything we can remember is stored in the preconscious mind. Anything we cannot recall or have trouble remembering is stored in the unconscious mind. Therefore preconsciousness is the reservoir of everything that we can remember voluntarily.

Often the memories that are stored in our preconscious mind have been repressed or suppressed in our conscious mind, yet can be recalled easily when given a cue. For example, a smell or song might remind you of a past lover, or a thought might trigger old emotional pain.

The Mind's Role

The Unconscious Mind

According to Freud, the unconscious mind is where we store every memory, experience, belief, and motivation, and these exist under the surface of conscious awareness. This is where hidden emotional attachments and repressed feelings are stored, along with hidden phobias and reactions, and automatic skills such as driving a car without being conscious of where you are driving. Also stored in the unconscious are the perceptions and beliefs that come from your education and experience, and all habits, good and bad.

You will identify with the roles shown below:

The Three Psychic Apparatuses

Now this is where it gets interesting. Freud introduced psychic apparatuses in the early 1900's as personality parts comprised of three components; the ID, Ego and Super-ego.

These apparatuses are functions of the mind rather than parts of the brain, and do not correspond one-to-one with the conscious, preconscious and unconscious minds, but instead overlap with them. They either belong within the conscious, preconscious or unconscious minds uniquely or can sway between them (see Figure 2).

Mind Chatter That Matters

Figure 2

The Mind's Role

The ID

Figure 3

The ID is the instinctive, generally inherited, part of the personality, and is usually uncoordinated. It is often referred to in psychology as the "child", remaining infantile throughout a person's life, always seeking instant gratification, inducing excitation and being driven by the "pleasure principal". The ID is responsible for satisfying your basic needs and desires.

This part of our personality structure contains our basic, instinctual drives and is present from birth. The ID is where our needs, desires, impulses, and sexual and aggressive drives lie. It seeks to avoid pain and gain pleasure.

Mind Chatter That Matters

According to Freud the ID is unconscious by definition:

"It is the dark, inaccessible part of our personality, what little we know of it we have learned from our study of dream work and of the construction of neurotic symptoms, and most of that is of a negative character and can be described only as a contrast to the ego. We approach the ID with analogies: we call it a chaos, a cauldron full of seething excitations... It is filled with energy reaching from the instincts, but it has no organisation, produces no collective will, but only a striving to bring about the satisfaction of the instinctual needs subject to the observance of the pleasure principle." [3]

To sum up the Child:
- Instinctive inherited personality
- Childlike
- Seeks instant gratification
- Responsible for satisfying your basic needs and desires
- Instinctual drives from birth
- Needs, desires, impulses and sexual drive lie with the Child
- Avoids pain and gains pleasure

The Mind's Role

The Super-ego

Figure 4

Freud developed his concept of the Super-ego from an earlier combination of the ego ideal and the "special psychical agency which performs the task of seeing that narcissistic satisfaction from the ego ideal is ensured ... what we call our 'conscience.'" [4]

The Super-ego is where we become moral beings. When it is developed it governs the ego like a governing parent, giving out orders, judging the Ego and ID and threatening them when they do not obey its orders. Thus it is often referred to as the "Parent."

Always watching over the decisions of the Ego and the demands of the ID, the Super-ego bombards us with criticism and punishes us with guilt, anxiety and inferiority.

The Super-ego takes the learned parental or cultural rules we have experienced and stored into our unconscious mind and applies those learnings to our Ego and ID. This is often done in a narcissistic voice because the Super-ego gains satisfaction from the controlling mechanisms used to aim for perfection. It operates – mainly unconsciously – to prohibit our ID's drives, fantasies, feelings and actions. With its ideals and spiritual beliefs, the Super-ego strives to guide us towards morally appropriate behaviour from its own perspective.

These moral judgments may be learned from principles and rules established by our cultural and parental education and perceptions, and act to remind us of the remorse we may feel when we commit actions that go against our values and the loss of integrity we feel when we don't adhere to our consciences.

Interestingly enough, Freud further adds "Conscience" as an aptitude, faculty, intuition or judgement for our moral compass, helping us distinguish right from wrong as part of the Super-ego.

To sum up the Parent:
- Governs like a parent to the Adult
- Gives out orders
- Judges the Adult and Child
- Threatens when Adult and Child do not follow its orders
- Bombards us with criticism, punishment of guilt, anxiety and inferiority

The Mind's Role

- Prohibits drives, fantasies, feelings and actions
- Learns parent or cultural rules and applies them
- Morally appropriate behaviour corresponding to its ideals and spiritual beliefs.

The Ego

Figure 5

The Ego is the executive of the personality and is governed by the "reality principle". It manages decision making and planning and is the responsible, logical part of the personality. The Ego learns as we grow and is able to determine the difference between a desire and reality – something that the ID cannot do – so is often referred to as the adult that mediates between the desires of the ID and the Super-ego.

The Ego seeks to please the ID's desire in realistic ways that will produce long term benefits. The Ego's regulating mechanism is used to delay gratification of the immediate needs of the ID; it engages in judgment, tolerance, reality testing, control, planning, defence, and synthesis of information, separating out what is real and what makes common sense. It tries to keep the balance between the ID and Super-ego, allowing some of the ID's desires to be expressed whilst still maintaining the individual's safety. It is often referred in psychology as the "Adult."

To sum up the Adult:
- Governed by the reality principle
- Determines between desire and reality
- Mediates between the desires of the Child and the Parent
- Seeks to please the needs of the Child in realistic ways
- Uses judgement, tolerance, testing, control and planning
- Tries to find balance and ensure the individual's safety
- Allows the Child's desires to be expressed.

The combination

Freud suggested that these three forms of psychic energy are generated by desires which come from a biological and a psychological need. Freud also believed that continuous psychic energy is generated, but that only a certain amount is available for use at any one point in time. This effectively means the Ego, Super-ego or ID never work

The Mind's Role

together – one always governs another.

Since the ID cannot distinguish between what is real or imagined, it may initiate any action to satisfy a need. However, the ID's psychic energy may be captured by the Ego and become associated with an Ego activity. For example, you see a car you would like to buy, you imagine yourself in the car, feeling great, and you decided to save or plan to purchase the car rather than going out and buying it immediately as your ID would propose.

At times the ID doesn't always distinguish between reality and fantasy and may act in ways that are not socially acceptable or realistic. Can you recall an occasion when you or somebody else displayed impulsive or antisocial behaviour?

Fortunately the Ego can repress the ID's undesirable thoughts or actions, and does step in to block irrational or immoral thoughts from the ID and ensure you act appropriately.

Still, there are times where the Ego cannot keep the ID's undesirables from coming to conscious awareness and being acted upon. It takes a lot of energy to repress certain desires and because there is only certain amount of psychic energy available the other processes may be short changed. For example, you are under pressure doing work you don't want to do but instead of quitting your job (the ID's undesirable thought) you instead go home and have quite a few alcoholic beverages or some food that makes you feel worse afterwards. The Ego rationalises that this course of action is better because at least you keep your job. In this way the ID's desires are contained but still expressed.

Mind Chatter That Matters

When the Super-ego gets involved with the negotiation between the ID and Ego it becomes a ball game. That's when Mind Chatter begins – when all psychic apparatuses try to battle for first place.

You end up with a desire, a parental voice and a mediator, with lots of unconscious stored influence pushing its own agenda.

No wonder we all look and act confused on a regular basis!

To sum up the combination:
- The Child has desires and pushes its own agenda
- The Parent pushes its own agenda, with criticism, guilt, moral judgement and belief systems
- The Adult struggles to find balance
- We decide on the best decision or direction forward based on experiences and conditioning, and how our ego minds stored these. You may find the following occurring:
  - Your Parent and Child fight for first place unconsciously
  - Self sabotage, depending on what part governs the decision
  - Self protective behaviour, and resistance of others' judgement
  - Self destructive behaviour, because the Child often governs the decisions
  - Avoidance of growth out of fear of more inner and outer condemnation
  - Blocks in our Collective Unconscious experience and understanding. More on this now.

The Mind's Role

A new understanding - Analytical Psychology

Carl Gustav Jung, (26 July 1875 – 6 June 1961) first met Sigmund Freud in Vienna in 1906. They influenced each other over the coming years and Freud referred to Jung as his "crown prince and successor". However, Jung had his own philosophy on psychology which de-emphasized the importance of Freud's libido theory and focused on the collective unconscious.

Jung travelled the world extensively and analysed the Eastern and Western cultures and their religions.

Later in his life Jung focused particularly on personality development, and believed a theory of mind must take into account the biological, spiritual and cultural aspects of a person's identity. He believed that psychic self-care was essential to the well-being of humankind.

Jung suggested that the psyche is comprised of three components: the ego, the personal unconscious and the collective unconscious. The ego represents the conscious mind, while the personal unconscious contains personal memories and experiences that may be repressed or suppressed. Jung believed that the collective unconscious serves as a form of psychological inheritance containing all the knowledge and experience we share as a species. It is where our memories are stored; including ideas inherited from our ancestors, and is the seat of our innate need for personal growth and our spiritual connections. Jung's proof of the vast collective unconscious was his theorised concept of synchronicity, that unexplainable and mysterious connectedness we all have with one another.

Mind Chatter That Matters

Jungian psychology, the school of psychology that originated from the ideas of Carl Jung, emphasises the attainment of the "Self" through individuation, the 'archetype of wholeness and the regulating centre of the psyche'. Jung believed that the human psyche is a self regulating adaptive system and that if thwarted, the energy stops flowing and regresses. The principals of Jung's theory are those of adaption, projection and compensation, which are essential to the psyche's ability to adapt.

Further to that Jung described the collective unconscious as holding fundamental questions of humanity; life, death, meaning, happiness and fear. It also encompasses spiritual concepts which become integrated into a person's psyche.

Jung's individuation concept means a person is transformed to become an individual and different from other human beings. This process is brought about by bringing a person to an awareness of their collective unconsciousness by way of dreams, active imagination or free association. Individuation then has a holistic healing effect.

Jung's concept of the individuation process is that it is where milestones are reached from the 'shadow' through to the 'Self', bringing clearer the uniqueness of oneself amongst other human beings.

Today's psychological and psychiatric specialists have been educated in both Jungian and Freudian theories and these are still taught in universities all around the world.

The Mind's Role

Figure 6

I believe that Freud and Jung theorised and documented the mind extremely well on a psychological level, and this book is designed to give you tools to better understand how your inner conflict operates and to help you find your own uniqueness as part of the collective unconscious that resides within you and the world.

The role of the collective unconscious may provide you with a sense of one or more of the following:
- Individuation from seeing and accepting your differences to others
- Seeing that this material world is not all there is
- Believing that there is more to this life
- Feeling connected to nature and its purpose

Mind Chatter That Matters

- Feeling a need to grow and develop – not for egotistical reasons
- Feeling a need to have a spiritual connection to a higher power
- A belief that synchronicity is real
- A belief that we are all connected to one another.

Next I explain how to unpack the confusion of your thoughts in order to gain better clarity on the Mind Chatter you experience. Later in the book you will learn tools to inner peace and how to gain the clarity you need to reduce the battles in your mind.

- CHAPTER 4 -

UNPACKING THE CONFUSION

"The pendulum of the mind alternates between sense and nonsense, not between right and wrong"

~ Carl Jung

How do we unpack the confusion when there seems to be so many voices in opposition to each other? When you begin to understand your mind's different voices, how they operate, what their individual intentions are, and what goals they are trying to fulfil, you will be better able to choose which voice should be honoured as a major part in the decision making.

In order to help you associate with theories used in Freudian and Jungian psychology from this chapter forward, I will refer to the ID as the *Child*, the Ego as the *Adult*, the Super-ego as the *Parent* and the Collective Unconscious as the *Intuitive Self*. This will improve your understanding of how your mind works and how you can unlock your mental blocks.

The Child part of our personality is an inherited part that makes each one of us as individual as our fingerprints. Its agenda is self-preservation to obtain the desired results; it is concerned only with fulfilling its own desires and needs, not worrying about respect, boundaries or consequences. It has an undeniable driving force of selfishness and goal seeking without justification, so much that it would drive you over a cliff to experience high speeds, with no thought of safety or any desire to save one's life.

The Child constantly seeks to satisfy its new goals—new hobbies, new jobs, new relationships, new endeavours and so on. The 'grass is greener' perception is driven by the Child. Although the Child is a selfish driving force, when tamed appropriately it can provide passion and purpose in your life.

However, since the Child reaches to obtain anything it wants, it can be the most destructive force in your life. I am sure you have experienced a time where your Child has been in charge, causing self-destructive or sabotaging behaviour that has wreaked havoc in your life.

Many people self-sabotage on a regular basis, continuing to observe themselves without truly understanding why they continue unhealthy relationships, unhappy employment and/or self abuse with food, alcohol, drugs and prescription medications. In these cases the Child is running the show, making the decisions whilst the Adult provides little or no mediation and the Parent has been

Unpacking the Confusion

suppressed or ignored. When a Child voice takes over because of the inner conflict and lack of psychic energy and Adult mediation, you are sure to continue on a self-destructive path.

To change this pattern of the Child's win and the Parent's loss, the Adult needs to step up with the help of the Intuitive Self. (More in Chapter 8). If the Adult does not step in at this time to mediate and instead simply observes as emotions elevate, and become so high between the Child and the Parent, the mind has only enough psychic energy for a win-lose result. If the Child wins it is often self sabotaging because the Child has no limits. When the Parent wins it suppresses the Child, which often makes the Child rebellious in other areas where it can win.

When this conflict occurs, the Parent voice becomes apparent with its judgements, condemnations, criticisms or guilt induction, and you need to become consciously aware of its negativity and unhelpful thoughts. It is time to tell the Parent to quieten, which is often a difficult task.

> *It is not who you were conditioned to be,*
> *but who you are destined to become.*

Depending on your life experience, conditioning and the information stored in your unconscious mind, your Parent voice may operate in a markedly different way to even those of your siblings or family members and friends. This is very apparent in children who have had different experiences within a family unit. Factors such as birth

Mind Chatter That Matters

order and family responsibilities may mean siblings have quite different unconscious conditioning.

Your Child may be spontaneous, creative, rebellious or adaptive, or a combination of any or all of these traits. It is important that we learn to express all parts of our Child to live a happy and fulfilled life with the supervision of our Parent, the regulation of our Adult and the direction of our Intuitive Self.

Your Adult may be committed, responsible, rigid or over cautious; it may resolve or avoid conflict, have real or unrealistic expectations, and either plan well or fail to plan. This role too is modelled to you and stored in your unconscious. It can be difficult to have your Adult step in and make the necessary decisions from a balanced and realistic point of view.

Your Parent's role is to supervise and give out orders, acting as a regulatory body to control the Child and Adult. What you have stored in your unconscious mind will determine the style of self parenting that you apply and the responsibilities that the Adult will take on. Parent roles can be nurturing, constructive or critical, and positive and negative attributes can be bundled together.

Having explained all that, most people take on negative or hurt experiences from events that have taken place in their lives, and store unhelpful beliefs into their unconscious. You are not alone, nor is it unfixable.

If you have experienced a mother, father or guardian that has been extremely loving and nurturing, or critical, controlling and

Unpacking the Confusion

abusive, then you may have internalised these roles into your unconscious mind. Some people experience both, with one parent being nurturing and the other abusive, so that conflicting parenting roles are experienced and stored. Every person stores unhelpful information into their unconscious mind.

Whatever your experience, you can learn to observe and govern your thoughts to reprogram your unconscious mind. Through becoming aware in the present moment of your mind chatter, you allow your Child some freedom to express its own individuality and passionate purpose, whilst maintaining control over the Parent directives and the Child's impulsivity. Everyone wins! This is how loving yourself can begin.

Your mind is your biggest asset or liability.
Use it wisely.

You may notice within your mind that you normally only hear two voices; the desires and demands of the Child and the criticisms and forcefulness of the Parent. When the Adult is in agreement and the Child is getting its needs met and the Parent has accepted the win-win situation, there is no conflict. When each of these two voices is actively playing it out to win its agenda, your Adult voice is observing and attempting to mediate between the Child and the Parent voice and only two voices appear.

The fourth voice, your Intuitive Self, can be difficult to hear when confusion and conflict reigns. Yet it is this voice that will give you the right direction to take.

Emotions and their role

Emotions are another layer and can be the driving force of decisions in your life. They can drive you to make the decisions you later regret or those that give you results you feel incredibly lucky to have obtained.

The Child's push to meet our needs to receive love and rewards will sometimes cause you to move mountains to obtain what are perceived as positive goals. But are they helpful goals or self-sabotaging behaviours intended to rebuke the Parent's over-controlling stance?

Fear

We can experience both positive and negative emotions on many levels, and fear is often the driving force that prevents us from moving forward. We can experience fear on many levels, including fear of success or failure, rejection, abandonment, loneliness and so on.

Fear paralyses most people, preventing them from making decisions that will allow them to move forward and honour the Child within.

Unpacking the Confusion

Figure 7

What fear do you live with on a daily basis? We often fear because we don't trust. We don't trust because our unconscious beliefs that have been stored from experiences have proven that we shouldn't trust. Yet your Child within will continue to push its own agenda regardless of your fears or your Parent's justifications for remaining within its comfort zone.

Fearful emotions can be triggered by any of your voices, which makes it often difficult to ascertain which voice to follow.

Whilst the Child has its own untamed passions and purpose, beliefs concerning your lack of trust in yourself and the world are upheld by the Parent. Fear can then appear to come from the Child because it can't get its needs met from the Parent because of its belief systems around its comfort zones, and from the Adult because it can't make a decision based on what seems to be valid information.

Mind Chatter That Matters

Between the Child's wants and needs and the Parent's inner critic, it is imperative that the Adult steps in to mediate between the Child and the Parent, with the support of the Intuitive Self. If the Adult does not step in at this time to mediate, and instead simply observes emotions elevate and become so high between the Child and the Parent, then the mind has only enough psychic energy to allow either the Parent or Child to win, with no negotiation and no win-win result. If the Child wins it is often self sabotaging. When the Parent wins it suppresses the Child.

How do we know when the Child has a fear of not being honoured and continues to self sabotage? The Parent's voice becomes very strong and tries to overrule the Child. The Child feels hurt and denied. When this stress is so high the Parent's unconscious beliefs cannot be challenged because its reasoning is buried in the hidden unconscious mind. The Parent prevents growth based on its previous experience and stored beliefs, so the Child continues to sabotage to get its needs or desires fulfilled, possibly in unhealthy ways because the Child feels hurt and unheard.

It is imperative that the Adult evaluates our emotions so as to recognise when either the Parent's or Child's agenda is negative. We need the Adult to hold the needs of that voice until a more appropriate decision can be made with the guidance of the Intuitive Self.

When emotions run high within it is difficult to distinguish between voices and identify who is running the show, making the decisions at our own peril.

Unpacking the Confusion

All people have a larger driving force towards either seeking pleasure or avoiding pain.

Depending on your experience and conditioning, if you lean more towards avoiding pain, your Parent will overrule and control your Child. If you are driven to seek pleasure over pain your Child will overrule your Parent.

Where is your adult in all of this? It's observing and being indecisive because the psychic energy resources are limited!

Emotions are natural and need to be felt, expressed, acknowledged and understood in order for them to contribute to our psychological growth and wellbeing.

If this process if thwarted, repressed or denied for any reason, this often results in distorted emotions which are unhealthy both psychologically and physically.

The information in Table 1 shows a variety of different emotions and is not conclusive. If your emotions have been repressed or suppressed by one psychic apparatus or another, you can start to work on your mind chatter.

Fear can be the common hand brake on your life. Fear prevents us from moving out of bad situations or experiences and conditioning. Your mind will try its best to prevent you from moving out of your 'uncomfortable' comfort zone. When thoughts arise about moving forward or in any direction, fear rises and overcomes the decision making process. Getting fear to take a back seat can sometimes be impossible, and the result is a no-win situation where the Child or Parent fights it out for first place.

Look through the table on the following page and see what you are feeling on a regular basis and take note of the stressful times in your life when you may have been living more from the distorted emotions rather than natural emotions.

	Natural Emotions	Distorted Emotions
Fear	Fight/Flight/Freeze impulse, cautious, startled.	Greed, obstinate, suspicious, over cautious, frightened, worry, anxious, petrified, panicked and phobias.
Love	Blissful, self-confident, giving and receiving, kindness, nurturing, emotional support and self-love.	Controlling, demanding, possessive, abandoned and dominating, inadequate, insecure, instability of love.
Anger	Used to bring about change, self protects, assertive and firm with self and others.	Rage, hatred, frustrated, bitterness, self-hate, resentment, aggressive, hurt, powerless, no inner authority, defeated, cheated and intimidated.
Jealous	Impels and motivates us to grown, improve out self worth, model from another person's behaviour	Envious, deceitful, criticism of self and others, competitive and comparative.
Grief	Sharing of feelings, loss and tears.	Depression, blame, regret, remorse, guilty, self-pity, martyrdom or suicidal.

Table 1

Unpacking the Confusion

Think back over your life and the more difficult times you have encountered. During those times of stress, pressure and upset, how did you respond? Did you move from the natural emotions over to being more distorted? Do you live more from distorted emotions in everyday life? This table is a fabulous gauge on how you are feeling and gives you the opportunity to see if you are responding to stresses from your stored experiences and conditioning in your unconscious mind, your survival response.

The emotion of fear retards our growth, preventing us from moving away from distorted emotions and making change in our lives. This is because we have been conditioned to be fearful. People go through pain, hardship and difficulties in life, some more than others. Depending on how we all reference these experiences and at what age determines how we overcome the distorted emotions. For example, an adult that has had wealthy upbringing may manage financial difficulties differently to one who has had conditioning of financial hardship in their childhood. Therefore one person may move out of the distorted emotions quickly when they recognise them, while another may become stuck because of resentment that others have had it so much better financially. You can become stuck in an 'uncomfortable' comfort zone and false security in order to prevent change. The ego mind will tell you that you have no need to change and that the world is unreliable and unproductive to you. Unfortunately, we have learnt from a very young age that our needs are met outside of ourselves and so the focus is on blaming the outside world for not providing what we need or want, rather than on the change that is needed and guided by the inner world of the Intuitive Self and a balanced approach of the Adult.

Love

Love is the opposite of fear and can easily wipe it out. Learning to love yourself from the inside and find your own internal resources will see your fears dissolving.

Letting go of your fears can be one of the most difficult things in life to do if you cling to your old unconscious conditioning. Fears are not only phobias but can be the basis of panic, anxiety and even depression. Fear of losing control of your life can overcome you, while fear of losing control over someone else's contribution to your life can prevent growth when you feel empty inside. Fear can destruct the relationships you are trying so hard to prevent losing. Being abandoned or not being valued or accepted are the two biggest motivators of fear. These most often originate in childhood conditioning, arising from simple gestures or protective comments from a parent such as, "You can't go out with those friends. They are all users" or "Put that knife down you will cut yourself", through to condemning statements such as "You will never be anything. You are useless".

Being aware of your biggest fear is a huge help in seeing the agenda of your Parent and Child.

Love is a natural state where we give and receive emotional support and nurturing, which results in us feeling happy.

We learn about love and its conditions in our childhood. People are generally taught to return love and respect to those who provide and protect, but are not taught how to love themselves. Mixed messages

Unpacking the Confusion

of love are absorbed into your unconscious. You are driven by these 'love' rules when you develop relationships with others.

Distorted love can make you clingy, needy, possessive, demanding and controlling. It can cause you to make statements that manipulate people into meeting your love needs. It can manifest in a person trying to seek love at all costs. Do you give too much and not love yourself enough? You may be giving too much love away in your attempts to receive love because you feel that is the only method of achieving love. You cannot give love to another unless it resides within you. You have this innate gift to love yourself and not seek your love needs outside. We are not always taught this.

Anger

Anger in its natural state is a very powerful emotion and is used to bring about change. When you, your values and beliefs are denied, anger expressed in an assertive manner serves to control someone's power over you. When someone is getting you to do something that you don't even want to do you become unhappy and you have every right to express anger. In doing this you are exercising self protection by being assertive and firm about what is right for you.

Unfortunately society does not encourage the natural expression of anger. Suppression of anger is expected among women and men because if we express anger we are labelled 'out of control'. This is a common misperception. Anger if expressed, brings about change. Suppressed anger brings about aggression, rage, bitterness, resentment, grudges and self hate as you turn your anger inwards.

Mind Chatter That Matters

Or it can make you feel powerless with no authority to bring about change. This learned pattern can be undone when you give yourself permission to express your values from an Adult voice with the support of your Intuitive Self!

Jealousy

Jealousy can provide you with the motivation to improve your life: it encourages you to emulate someone else who is living a more positive life. Finding an inspiring person to look up to is using jealousy in a natural state. When jealousy becomes distorted you become consumed by envy, competitiveness, and constantly compare yourself to others. Your perceived lack quickly converts into low self-worth and low self-esteem. Do not fall into the trap of comparing your unique self with others!

Grief

Grief... along with fear, it is one of life's most difficult of emotions to process and let go of. If you have experienced grief on any level, you will know it can and does consume you at times. It feels like the pain shall never resolve, especially when you lose someone in this world through death or severed relationships. To deal with grief naturally, it is imperative to share your sadness and loss with others, be they friends, family or counsellors. Grief is a natural emotion. If you are lucky enough to grow into a mature age you will endure grief at some stage. When grief occurs your expectation of the way your world was supposed to look becomes shattered. You have no control

Unpacking the Confusion

in getting that world back. Grief can drive you into desperation to stop the pain. This shattering of what feels like your entire being is the shattering of your mind's projected future, believing that nothing will change.

Society doesn't support grieving very well—people don't know how to support someone in their grief. Thus expressions of grief are commonly met with "Don't cry", when tears and sharing is a natural way to express grief. Expressing grief will reduce your length of suffering and ill health may result if you repress this powerful emotion. Find someone who can listen and watch you grieve to enable you to move through your pain as fast as possible.

Men in particular are conditioned to believe that crying shows their weakness to their women, their families and to other men. There is an instinctual drive to avoid being seen as weak/inferior amongst the wolf pack. Feelings of inadequacy can prevail when a man perceives himself as weak.

If burying your grief seems a better option than dealing with the insurmountable pain, be very careful, as grief buried will become distorted very quickly. You will then be dealing with more negative emotions on top of your grief!

You may at times get stuck in grief—feeling cheated, guilty. You may feel regret and blame that can result in a downward spiral of depressive feelings. You may become a martyr because of your guilt or regret, allowing others to walk all over you while you give too much of yourself.

Awareness and acceptance that change is a given in this world will help you deal with grief. Grief exposes you emotionally and makes you vulnerable, which is difficult for some. To process grief is to process a new acceptance of what life now is, with your loss. To blame yourself for not doing enough or spending more time with someone you lost will prevent you from grieving. Self-acceptance and self-forgiveness is needed if things weren't done differently on your part.

Whatever you have been through—and I know some people have been through the most horrendous and difficult times because of the decisions or actions of themselves and others—you can recover from your experiences, conditioning and the references you have stored in your unconscious mind. You have the power to change it!

The inadequate and inferior mask

Whatever you do, do not fall into the trap of comparing your inside emotions to everyone else's outside mask.

When we measure ourselves against others we feel inadequate because we're only looking at the mask that their psyche portrays to the world, and a lot more is hidden inside. Their psyche manages to hide its inadequacies and negative distorted emotions behind its mask to prevent judgement from others.

The mask is worn by a majority of people in order for them to feel secure and adequate in the eyes of others so as to avoid rejection or abandonment and a malady of other negative emotions.

Unpacking the Confusion

Figure 8

We measure ourselves against other people in the world without considering what life experience or conditioning they have stored into their unconscious minds and what lays hidden from view. Haven't you ever met a person only to find out that your perception of them has changed dramatically? It is not your perception at fault, but that their mask has fallen off.

The thicker a mask, the more there is to hide. The ironic misunderstanding, that we all have, is that innately we all sense when someone is not being their true self. Bells ring, flags fly and we ignore our Intuitive Self. We tend to overlook these senses until we understand the mask concept and learn to trust our instincts.

Everyone has events in their life that are painful on some level. We are rejected in employment, stolen from, and dumped in relationships; adultery is committed; deceit, abuse, rape and manipulation of people occurs. Sometimes through no fault of our own we experience suffering at the hands of another. But how do

Mind Chatter That Matters

we react to this? We immediately feel an injustice. This injustice is measured by our Parent's default settings—its morals and beliefs concerning how we should be treated. So whether or not you accept the injustice and move on depends on your Parent's opinion of the injustice.

For example, many of my clients have high levels of emotional sensitivity, kindness and loving ability, and when injustice is done to them they struggle to understand this poor treatment. When these types of people are hurt in this manner, they suffer greatly, as their Parent's role is loving and nurturing others, and it cannot comprehend how another person can be so callous and uncaring of another. They feel great pain because they believe they failed themselves in not having protected themselves against the injustice, and, because they simply do not operate in a hurtful manner towards others, they also fail to understand the cruelty of the injustice. The more experienced 'hurt' people tend to nurture themselves throughout the injustice or hold their injustice on the inside where it becomes distorted to project their pain and label the world cruel and hopeless.

Are you stuck on a bad reaction to something painful that someone else did to you? Are you suffering from being victimised by someone who may still be in your life or has left it completely? When we hold onto emotions and pain, we hurt ourselves. Suffering is an indicator that someone has wronged you. Feeling like a victim is a difficult position to live in, especially when you feel like the world is against you. It can be difficult to move on from victimhood to a place of personal power when we are stuck in hurt and pain. When you are victimised time and time again, it can be a struggle to see the future ahead without a dark cloud of powerlessness hanging over you. We worry about our future, not knowing how to shift our inner conflict, and can't seem to shake being a victim. Once again this is distorted anger.

How do we overcome this suffering? By simply telling it like it is…it is all in your thinking. They are your thoughts and the total sum of your thoughts is an important component of who you are. It is time to own your thoughts, regardless of who is at fault for putting them there. But remember you are more than just your thoughts!

Anxiety

Anxiety and worry are fears. They are fears about the inability to control the outcome of an event or its effect on a person. When we worry, we are living in a moment that has not yet occurred in the future. We imagine and project a scene into a movie or event that may or may not occur. As we do this we are not present in our conscious mind, and we are feeding fear into our unconscious mind, reinforcing beliefs that the world is full of negative and hurtful experiences. Our belief in not trusting is proven again. Become aware of your anxieties and worries as often as possible. Bring them into your conscious mind and get your Adult to work! Your Adult has the ability to overrule this style of thinking. Very stressful situations and the worrying they bring about can stop you from thinking rationally and responsibly. When you learn to become conscious or mindful, you can control these thoughts too!

Depression

Depression can be caused by many things in a person's life and is often accompanied by chemical changes in the brain. These chemical imbalances can be caused by many things, including a genetic predisposition, drugs, prescription medications, alcohol, intolerances and allergies from your food or the environment.

I do not profess to be an expert on depression and do not wish to dismiss depression in any way, as I too have suffered from depression. For me it was my thinking patterns causing my troubles and negative thoughts, together with blocks where I couldn't resolve issues. I needed help and sought it.

I am never going to dismiss the heavy heart and mind depression causes to its sufferers. The major purpose for writing this book is to inspire others to move forward, away from painful thinking and the possibility of sinking into deep depression and taking their own lives.

Figure 9

Unpacking the Confusion

Depression and suicide are difficult topics to discuss, whether you are the victim or not. Victims of depression suffer from a huge sense of failure. They find discussing their failure to others makes them even more vulnerable. Victims feel as though they have failed in the past and that they are useless in their present; they have no vision for the future.

Depression can hit suddenly or you can gradually slide downhill only to realise that you are severely depressed. If you are the victim of depression, it can be rectified. When the chemical imbalance occurs in your brain it can be difficult to turn your thinking around to increase the 'feel good' chemicals and regain your psychological balance. While the tools in this book may assist you to change your thinking patterns, if you feel depressed you should be assessed by a medical practitioner.

Remember, every person on this planet called Earth is always valued by someone even, if they cannot feel it right at this moment. You are never alone, even if you feel alone with your troubles. I know at times it feels that you have no one and that you have failed the world, but the loss of your life will affect someone! When people suicide it leaves a massive hole in the heart of the people left behind, wishing they could have helped someone with depression or done something different for them. Even just a little. A touch, or a glance of hope and love is sometimes all you need just to keep your hope alive and kicking. Things change, that is a given in this world. There will be days you can reflect on that were happier than your down days. Hold onto those moments even if they seem like a sliver.

Depression doesn't need to be a silent killer. It doesn't need to be hidden, nor do your failures. We all fail on some level and often on many levels. When you compare your life from an internal perspective against another's external mask of confidence and success, you are cheating yourself of the truth that we all suffer some feelings of inadequacy or lack of self-worth. Everyone struggles with something on some level.

Support with anti-depressant medication is extremely helpful to correct your brain's chemical imbalance, and finding a supportive person to talk to will shine the light on your path and give hope back to your life.

In Australia alone, the suicide rates have reached a 10 year peak. It is estimated that 30% of depression sufferers are suicidal. The Australian Bureau of Statistics 2012 results are overwhelming: 16.8 of every 100,000 Males in Australia and 5.6 of every 100,000 Females in Australia commit suicide, which equates to almost 7 suicide deaths each day, almost twice as many as road related deaths. For every suicide at least 30 more are attempted each day, totalling around 200 attempts each day. It is also estimated that around 1,000 people think about suicide every day! [5]

These figures are astounding. Reach out if you know someone is suffering from prolonged sadness or depression. Just ask them if they feel like they are going to harm themselves or if they are feeling so low they cannot go on. This lifeline of caring gives the sufferers hope that someone cares and that they are not alone in their darkness and despair. You can make a huge difference. If a person admits they are considering self harm, stay with them until they get professional help. Don't leave them alone. You need to help and

Unpacking the Confusion

support them. Help is available everywhere. Doctors and hospitals are a good start, as is phoning a telephone support service such as Lifeline in Australia. It is much easier for the sufferers when they know someone cares enough to help lead the way. Be their beacon of light and hope.

I, and many of my clients, have suffered depression. It is like a big dark cloud where you lose hope of your present and future. Once I discovered it was in my thinking, I needed to find a different way of thinking.

My analogy for depression is "The inability to accept life as it is.... It doesn't look good right now and I am very sad about it. I want change, but I am stuck and don't know how. I feel hopeless and unable to see what I need to do". You have a definitive view on how your life should be and when you're depressed it's possibly looking very different from the way you would like it to be.

Life happens, experiences happen, and how we think about these makes all the difference. The experience of depression can take your life on a downward spiral, and there are times when you simply cannot see a way out and can't get back to the expectation you have of your life.

Depression can be caused by many things, but very often life's experiences are the trigger for a depressive bout, especially if we think our life should be a certain way and it simply isn't. We become disempowered by the inner conflict, and often a very critical and judgmental Parent voice takes over. Then the chemicals in the brain become unbalanced and we start to spiral down into depression.

Lucy arrived in my office very despondent that she had lost her job of two years. Lucy was a diligent employee and had had a new manager cease her employment upon his arrival without a thorough explanation. Lucy immediately questioned her self-worth. Lucy's Parent voice became very active to tell her that she was useless and unemployable. She struggled to feel confident enough to apply for other jobs. Her ability to be positive dropped and she slowly fell into depression. In her consultation we discovered that her mother had been always very critical and judgemental of Lucy's ability to earn pocket money doing cleaning jobs around the home. This was the block. Lucy had internalised this voice and had begun to do the same critical parenting job on herself. I could see her skills and we spoke of her positive attributes. Lucy gained confidence when she understood her inner conflict and earned herself a new job the following week.

You are more than your thoughts and emotions

Before we go on, I want you to just stop and think. You have all these voices, emotions, learned roles, stored experiences and conditioning, but can you feel you are more that those? Can you feel that you have another driving force within you? When you are in conflict with your mind chatter, you feel like you are your thoughts. When emotions are running high, you feel like you are only those emotions, but when they settle who are you? You are not your emotions, thoughts or experiences. You are you. You can only sense YOU when you are present in your conscious mind. In this state you can become aware of everything about you. Your arms,

Unpacking the Confusion

legs, body and even your beating heart. Your emotions and thoughts are separate to you. The driving force within you is your Intuitive Self, and that's who you are. The Intuitive Self is not an inner self that is present in your body, not your Child, Adult, Parent, pre- or unconscious experiences, nor is it in your conscious mind; however your conscious mind can become aware of your Intuitive Self.

So much of the time people are so busy thinking and doing that they forget about themselves in their movie of life. Observe your thoughts and decide who has got the steering wheel to ascertain who is driving the vehicle of your life. You can overcome your thoughts and get your new map out to drive yourself to happiness with purpose and passion.

First you must acknowledge all your thoughts, the good, bad and downright ugly. Without judgment or self-criticism (tell your Parent to shut up) look at all the different voices and pay attention to the negative unhelpful ones.

If you struggle to dig up your dirty laundry and hang it on the line for you to view in your conscious awareness, I suggest getting some counselling by a trained psychologist.

Psychology is an excellent way of learning how to hear the agendas of your Child and Parent so that you can allow the Adult to take action. Some people never operate from their Adult voice, and this can be seen, for example, in some children if their parents or guardians never allow them to have a voice of reason as they mature. For others the parent or guardian's critical voice of condemnation is so internalised they are paralysed with fear, unable to face disapproval

Mind Chatter That Matters

from anyone in the outside world, let alone self-criticism.

Seeing a psychologist will give you hope because someone is finally listening to you and understanding how you feel even if it doesn't make sense to you at the time. It helps when you have a better understanding of how you have stored or suppressed emotions and experiences, as this helps you become aware of some of your self-sabotaging or unconscious behaviours. It helps when you see your inner war and the pain and suffering that needs to be dealt with. It also helps when you understand the pain that has been passed through the generations of your family. Although psychology can be a long and expensive process, it will provide you with a relationship where a positive Parent and a rational Adult is modelled and internalised by the nurturing relationship with your practitioner. When making a decision on whom you are going to share your story with, ensure that you sense a trustworthy connection with your practitioner. If you have trouble making a connection, see if your Parent or Child is preventing change, because it is safer to project your blame and pain out in the world, onto some other person or situation. At the end of each day, you are living in your mind; no one else is there, just you. You need to live with you. Everyone else can get reprieve from your thoughts. You know how your thoughts work or don't work for you. You can become aware of your blaming thoughts and move on from them. Sometimes seeking an extra pair of eyes and ears makes all the difference.

It's imperative to be present in your conscious mind so that you can sort through your thinking and experiences. In Chapter 5 you will read more on the blame game and later, in Chapter 6, you will learn tools to be more present and to become more aware.

Unpacking the Confusion

Hope is everything. Hope comes from leaving the doors of your mind open! In Chapter 8, I explain how another voice, your Intuitive Self, can help you when you learn to listen to it and honour who you truly are and what you are meant to be doing on this earth. I believe hope and knowing is driven from this voice. This voice has your answers!

I will finish this chapter with this poem, which I think is a wonderful representation of the process of awareness and change:

> *I walk down the street*
> *There is a deep hole in the sidewalk*
> *I fall in*
> *I am lost...I am hopeless*
> *It isn't my fault*
>
> *I walk down the same street*
> *There is a deep hole in the sidewalk*
> *I pretend I don't see it*
> *I fall in again*
> *I can't believe I'm in the same place*
> *But it isn't my fault*
> *It still takes a long time to get out*
>
> *I walk down the same street*
> *There is a deep hole in the sidewalk*
> *I see it there*
> *I still fall in...it's a habit*
> *My eyes are open*

Mind Chatter That Matters

I know where I am
It is my fault
I get out immediately

I walk down the same street
There is a deep hole in the sidewalk
I walk around it

I walk down another street.

                                            Author Unknown.

Be gentle with yourself. You are worth it!

- Chapter 5 -

YOUR BELIEFS & VALUES

"The shoe that fits one person pinches another; there is no recipe for living that suits all cases"

~ Carl Jung

When we are born we are totally innocent about how the world works. We all have to learn and adapt to our unique set of circumstances. At an extremely young age we learn that all our needs are filled by external sources, normally by our parents or guardians. We are given food, nurturing and caring by others, as we are not able to meet these needs ourselves while still very young.

Abraham Maslow, an American psychologist, in 1943 developed "A Theory of Human Motivation". This is now commonly known as Maslow's Theory of self-actualisation and is taught in universities worldwide. Maslow's theory clearly shows how the levels of personal growth are required. The first tier of the theory shows that we need air, water, food, shelter, sleep and sex to survive as a species. These basic needs are provided by our caretakers at a very early age, together with the second tier of safety and security, and often the third tier of love and a sense of belonging (see Figure 10).

Maslow's theory details the layers humans need to work through to find one's self or self-actualisation. In all species of our planet a newborn provokes a natural caretaking instinct to provide for and protect the young. Innocence is a natural predisposition we are gifted with at birth. This innocence is thwarted by our caretakers without intention, as they do the best job they can with their abilities, knowledge and experience.

According to Maslow, when our basic instincts to survive are met we then move to find a safe and secure environment to live, then to feel loved and a have sense of belonging. Safety and security is generally met by our families or communities, whom I will call a Tribe. Tribes initially provide us with our sense of belonging and being cared for, regardless of whether we live with our blood relatives or are adopted, orphaned or fostered into families. When safety and security, love and belonging needs are not met because of war or natural disasters or economic crisis, or family violence and childhood abuse, children are less resourceful and more likely to feel the impact when not provided for by the tribe. Depending on the duration of the period where needs were not being met or taken care of, the child may be conditioned to deserving less or expecting less, which may result in a person finding it difficult to receive any of these needs. The opposite may also occur when a child has these needs provided and continues to demand their needs be met by the tribe on a consistent basis, even in adulthood.

Because we have been conditioned to externalise our needs, we learn to believe that all our needs are resolved outside of ourselves, and this is normal for every human being whilst growing up, regardless of the level to which our tribe has been self-actualised.

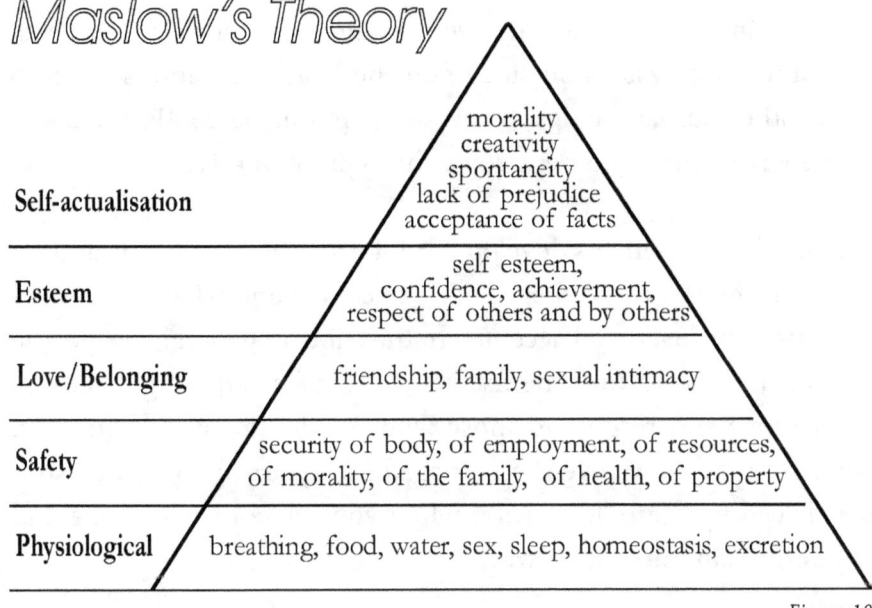

Figure 10

Our tribe's own journey through Maslow's theory to "Self-actualisation" will greatly affect our experience and conditioning. Therefore we become a reflection of their (the tribe's) experience, unless we choose otherwise.

This conditioning is what I refer to as *Tribal Consciousness*, where we are conditioned to believe and value the family, cultural, community, city, country, village or tribal rule of our upbringing

Mind Chatter That Matters

and environment. This tribal conditioning creates the beliefs and values which are stored into your unconscious mind, and they become your truth about your world. These perceptions you form and rely upon when referencing decisions and experiences are the product of your belief and value system.

During this process these tribal influencers, merely as caretakers without intention, make us feel certain that all that we need, including love, resides outside of our body and self and is given to us by other human beings. It is instilled in our perception that our needs will be met by other people throughout our lives.

These tribal influencers develop our internalised world view and we form a self deserving belief of what to expect and what is expected from us to be loved and accepted in the tribe. In general, few people are taught how to love themselves. Most of us are taught only to return love and respect to those who provide for and protect us. Mixed messages of love are absorbed into your unconscious. You are driven by these 'love' rules when you relate to your tribe and with others in the outside world.

We are taught to rely on our tribe during childhood and not to seek our needs or refuge elsewhere. When young, our tribe doesn't trust that we have yet internalised tools to survive and protect ourselves and we are taught not to rely on our own resources, which further implants the belief that our needs are always met externally. This is based on fear and fact. Tribes should provide for and protect their children to ensure they grow into well balanced, mature adults. However, each person's experience is different, even within the same tribe. One may internalise a safe environment and while another

Your Beliefs & Values

internalises an unsafe one.

Different skills of survival are learnt and internalised, to later be used in the world. As you mature you soon learn that others' beliefs and values are very different to yours. As we grow into adults and attempt to move out of our tribes and into the world, we often struggle with the differences of the new people in our lives; to find a new sense of belonging we learn to adapt in order to be acknowledged and accepted.

We are quick to adapt to the world outside of our tribe, and we continue to do whatever is necessary to fit into an outside world while maintaining our internalised beliefs and values. We measure and judge everyone, including ourselves. We establish who can meet our needs and set about the task of obtaining those needs externally.

This is where we all begin down a path of seeking to resolve our needs through people who may have different values and beliefs, and this can become a fruitless, hurtful and disappointing task.

We begin to measure ourselves against everyone else's mask and feel inferior. Survival of the greatest takes on a whole new meaning when we view the world as competitive. Meanwhile our internal world becomes more critical, demanding and guilt inducing.

We can fall into the pattern of looking for love and acceptance in all the wrong places; we form unhealthy friendships and relationships, falling victim to controlling teachers and bullies at school and in the workplace. The reasons we don't move away from those that hurt or control us is because they are making a contribution to our lives—we

Mind Chatter That Matters

are seeking, unsuccessfully, to receive the love, nurturing, security and safety we seek from these people (as we possibly previously obtained in our tribe).

Unfortunately, we do not always experience happiness in relationships. We may repeat a pattern of being in unhappy relationships, until we realise that loving others can often hurt. A relationship, though it may provide the comfort we seek, may bring more pain than being alone, because we are still seeking our needs to be met outside of ourselves.

When we've experienced a time when our basic needs weren't met by our tribe, we internalise a lack of worth and continue to seek these basic needs outside ourselves until we learn to become resourceful and meet these needs from within.

On top of having a Child voice out of control, and a critical or abusive Parent voice, we also have a driving instinctual force to survive and so we are looking to others that do not have all the answers, because of their Tribal Consciousness. No wonder we all walk around dazed and behind a mask!

Remember your innocence as a baby? You still have that innocence and you now have the opportunity to turn your conditioning around to anything you want.

Do your beliefs and values help or hinder you? Most people have something that they would love to change about themselves. Control over your weight, smoking, drug use, alcohol use, exercise, relationships, harshness or softness is obtainable—you just have to

Your Beliefs & Values

change your thinking.

You need to examine your beliefs and values, as they may be your truth today but not tomorrow. Have you not had a time when you were adamant about something and later changed your mind? Now is no different! No matter how negative your experience may have been, no trauma can control your beliefs. Beliefs are changeable. Remember your innocence as a newborn, young, loveable and full of joy, and understand that this innocence still resides within you now and can be your biggest asset to seeing yourself as a human being who deserved the best (even if you didn't receive it). If you believe you don't deserve anything then you are right—you don't! But the reverse is also true. A sense of deserving is everything. How were you conditioned to deserving? Are you angry you didn't get what you deserved as a child or adult? If not, get angry and use the anger positively to bring about the change you want! Remember not to slip into distorted emotions and don't give up your power or seek someone else to make the change for you. Make the difference to your life. We all deserve love and happiness. The decision starts with you. No one else. Make the decision now to get what you deserve, and I will show you how to bring about the change you want in the following chapters.

Who's to blame?

Should we blame our tribe if they were the ones who taught us everything? And if they are to blame, who do they blame? And who do the people they blame, blame again in return? It's generational thinking. Depending on your experience, you may have many

Mind Chatter That Matters

generations to blame. But wait one minute, is it right to blame generations of our tribe when we belong to them and they are our safety and security? That is like shooting yourself in the foot whilst trying to win the race of life.

Let's just go over the fact; your tribe raised you and taught you only what they knew of the ways of their world, but now this knowledge doesn't work for you. Blaming the tribe gives away your power to change your own personal thinking. How can you blame everyone else, when you are now the one with the thinking and the one with the power to change it?

Your awareness of the tribal brainwashing you received can be your greatest asset, biggest liability or both. Either way, you will always need to be aware of your Child, Adult, Parent and Intuitive Self voices in order to consistently make the new choices that will allow you to grow away from your old limiting beliefs and adopt those that are helpful and supportive. The tribe or world is not at fault for not giving you what you need, you were just led to believe this in your youth. You are now on your own, with the ability to create your own world and experience. No relationship or friendship can meet your needs, no employer can fulfil your career, no teacher can teach you everything, and a society is not at fault for your misdemeanours. The future lays in your hands, your actions and your thinking.

When you realise that your beliefs and values are yours—you own them—you get to steer your own vehicle and drive your life in exactly the direction you want.

Blaming your parents for the crappy upbringing will bring you no

Your Beliefs & Values

further joy, but instead will keep you locked into expecting them to change to make you happy. You externalise your power of happiness if you wait for the rest of your life to change. Some people never change. They get stuck and cannot move for fear of losing what little safety or security they have. Change becomes impossible for these blamers. Stop waiting for the world to make you feel better. It is now your responsibility.

Romantic relationships and friendships are a certainty in your life. Some may stay for a very short period, others a lifetime. What you have to offer a relationship should be a mirror of healthy behaviour, not a need for security or a desire to feel whole through the other person. But most of us seek security in our early years, giving of ourselves but not feeling better and more whole through the relationship as we expected. So who is at fault when our needs are not met? We are, because we are expecting our needs to be met outside of us. What would happen if we were not taught to have this expectation? How do we learn to meet our own needs of love, safety and security? We must learn to find ourselves through our Intuitive Self, not through our tribe or relationships.

Other tribes may appear more supportive and can become a better tribe for you than the one you have experienced previously. For example, many young teenagers who are victims of family abuse or neglect move to another tribe, such as a gang or bike club, to meet their need for belonging. Other relationships may appear better, and you can jump from one to another trying to fill up the void inside, only to be hurt and disappointed time and time again. Finding a role model that exhibits positive belief systems is imperative for your personal growth, but does not always need to result in you

Mind Chatter That Matters

disowning your current tribe or relationship.

As we mature we sometimes become wiser and realise that our parents or guardians could not provide all of our physical, emotional or financial needs because of their difficulties and conditioning in life and lack of ability to make their own changes. Often becoming a parent ourselves is what changes our outlook: we stop blaming our tribe and forgiveness can begin.

When we believe our tribe is right, we can also become rigid in our thinking, believing other tribes are wrong in regards to their living standards, cultures and religious beliefs. We see many different tribal wars in our world, tremendous clashes between rigid and self-righteous factions, which could be avoided if only our differences were acknowledged and accepted. This is a sad and destructive state for those locked into the rigid belief systems, and becomes a generational pattern instilled into the children. Hopefully the masses of people can help to heal these generational tribal patterns over time, to show these tribes a better way by providing freedom of thought and teaching self-love, which later turns to loving others regardless of race, creed or culture.

So respect your tribe, your experience, your conditioning, because it is yours, no one else's. It has given you a certain set of circumstances for your learning that have made you into who you are today. Someone did their best job at the time, with their knowledge, ability and experience, even if it wasn't up to your expectations or didn't compare favourably to others in the world. Your thinking is yours NOW and you have the power to CHANGE IT! Your mind is your power!

- CHAPTER 6 -

YOUR BLOCKS

*"Until you make the unconscious conscious,
it will direct your life and you will call it fate"*
~ *Carl Jung*

Being blocked is the state of not being aware and able to make conscious decisions about your life. We all get partially blocked sometimes, while at other times we can be completely blocked.

In the last chapter I explained how we become a by-product of conditioning and our tribal consciousness. When we want to unravel the learnt belief systems we need to be gentle on ourselves. It can be a difficult and painstaking task to review your faults and insecurities in your conscious mind whilst having your Parent's critical and condemning voice run into overdrive.

You need to see yourself from a perspective of your innocence, with an awareness of how you were conditioned, and you need to give yourself the space to learn to grow. This is a process of self love and forgiveness. If you do not look at your faults you cannot make judgement on what beliefs have held you back and what needs to change. This can be an overwhelming process at times, and although you may take one step forward and two back, you must be strong and not give up.

Accountability and responsibility

Your Parent may encourage you to avoid any accountability for the position of your unconscious mind's storage from your life experience up until now. This will sabotage your growth.

Your mind. Your thoughts. Your experience. Ownership will be your first step forward. You may not see the whole point of change and may find it too difficult to do. This is a copout. Pretending you don't need to change is a block, even though you can hear the need deep within you. Your conscious mind will be aware of what you need to change but has no idea where to start. I often refer to this as a can of worms. If it gets opened, there is no way to stop those little worms from escaping. There is no turning back. It is easier to deny the can and the worms, than to ever open the can and deal with everything! However you will know when you need change and your life isn't working because you will hear the request or need and suppress or deny it. Often you'll feel a fogginess about your future direction or confusion reigns in your thinking. Let's face it—change is difficult.

Your Blocks

The first step is to be accountable for the thoughts you continue to have. Be aware of them, no matter how difficult they are to see and how dark they appear, or how much of a failure you feel. These are only thoughts and you are more than your thoughts and feelings!

You need to take little steps. Treat yourself with kindness. You wouldn't kick a little child trying to walk if they didn't succeed the first or second time. Give yourself encouragement and support, just as you would a child. Don't let your Parent become critical and judgemental only to give up. Push the Parents voice back into the corner, pick yourself up and keep going.

Blind Spots in your Awareness

Ever had the experience where you kept trying to look at something to see what was there, but just weren't able see it, no matter how hard you tried? You were aware there was a gap in your awareness. Your understanding can have a blind spot. It's like driving a car and looking in your review mirror and seeing nothing but knowing a car is driving in your blind spot. You have to look again and again until you are certain something is there, otherwise you ignore the car. Just like this type of blind spot whilst driving your vehicle, a blind spot can reside in your awareness.

If you can sense or see a blind spot in your awareness, you may have what I call a self-protective block, where you can sense a black hole in your thinking and cannot quite catch what drives you from or prevents you from understanding. This is your mind's inability to resurface your unconscious mind's conditioning. It is keeping

Mind Chatter That Matters

that conditioning nice and safe from change. If it cannot be seen, it cannot be changed. The reason for your blind spot may be to prevent changes to your belief systems, therefore keeping your ego mind safe from change. This I believe is a safety mechanism that your ego mind maintains to prevent change of its certainty, and this can be a very destructive force of avoiding accountability and responsibility for our thoughts. Alternatively it is a safety mechanism to prevent more confrontation that the ego mind can deal with at any one time. It is a sure sign that your block is holding you in denial of the awareness of your thoughts. A safety mechanism like this can deny you growth and happiness, as not confronting your belief systems can hold you back on every level. Welcome the awareness and allow yourself to see all your faulty thoughts and belief systems. This will bring change in your life as you lift these blind spots and blocks.

When you begin to analyse your behaviour, reasons for your decisions and the consequences of those decisions, you can generally view the faulty beliefs that do not work towards your happiness. This process shines a spotlight onto your blind spot and awareness occurs. The more you do this, the fewer blind spots you have. Willingness to look is the answer to reducing these blind spots, as this allows the Intuitive Self to show you what needs to be changed to grow.

Bill, a client of mine, needed to change his job as he was bored, unhappy, dissatisfied and felt underpaid for the sacrifice he made in being away from his family. It was definitely time to move jobs. Although he clearly needed a change, he couldn't figure out why he just couldn't look for another job and resign from his unfulfilling job. No matter how difficult it was, he didn't resign. He became more and more unhappy until depression set in. It affected all his life, and he

Your Blocks

began drinking to relieve the pressure and unhappiness. His block was that he had been conditioned through his childhood to avoid poverty and lack, therefore he was putting money before wellbeing and happiness. However, his depression and drinking affected his work performance and this led to him being sacked, leaving him in a powerless position both financially and emotionally, exactly the same position he was trying to avoid. His self-protective block had provided his self-fulfilling prophecy.

Bill had a battle within: the Child who wanted to move on and find another job to bring happiness into his life was held back by the Parent who forced him into a position of providing security. The Parent voice was so strong the Adult couldn't even see the rational way out. The Child became depressed and eventually got what it so desperately needed...to be free of that job!

Another client, Jane, came to see me with a history of abusive and neglectful relationships. She had jumped from one relationship to another, wanting to give love and hopefully receive it. Jane's family upbringing was one of family violence at the hands of her occasionally abusive father. However, because her brother also became cruel and abusive to her this further reinforced her lack of self-worth and validated a belief system that told her she must earn love from men. When Jane kept attempting to heal her lovers with her unconditional love, she was consistently hurt because she couldn't see how giving all her love away to abusive lovers was hurting her. Her self-protective block prevented her from seeing her own lack of self-worth as she focused on fixing other people, men who needed to find a better way of relating. When Jane finally realised the problem was with her conditioning and the beliefs she had upheld all her life, her life changed for the better. She took accountability for her mistakes and her conditioning and responsibility for loving herself followed. Her growth was wonderful to watch.

Looking outside for your answers

You can experience pain and hurt and may blame someone else, especially if that person has wronged you terribly. Do not get caught up in blaming someone for your pain. No one can hurt you without your permission. This can be difficult and confronting to understand when you are in pain. To explain, it is your thoughts about the actions of others that create your pain. You either own what they have done or you don't. It becomes a part of you or it doesn't. If it wasn't your actions that were hurtful, don't let them cause you pain. When you choose to see the perpetrator as another human in pain, you keep your power and can respond with the appropriate action to protect yourself if needed. Liking or loving another doesn't mean you have to accept their bad or hurtful behaviours. Instead you need to get angry in a positive way and bring about change to their treatment of you; don't become full of rage, powerless or anything in between.

Drama doesn't just walk into your life out of nowhere; you either create it, invite it, or associate with people that bring it.
Frankie John.

Your Blocks

Every time you feel a reaction to someone, there is an emotive reactive thought that travels at the speed of light through your mind and activates you to respond in action or defence from your unconscious conditioning. This emotive thought is often difficult to be aware of, but awareness is key to preventing you from reacting and losing your balance. Your emotions drive you to protect yourself, and it is often the distorted emotions which are triggered due to the Parent responding to fear-based conditioning. When you become aware of the emotive thought your Adult voice can step in.

Projecting the blame and pain is a block. Your Parent is blocking your growth and change based on fear or beliefs of prior experience. Evaluate what your fear is or what you do not want to acknowledge in your blocks. History is a perfect science. Look at your history and consider your beliefs, decisions and the consequences of your thoughts and actions. Your Parent voice will hold this information under lock and key, buried safe in the deepest part of your mind. You can unlock this with ease with the help of your Intuitive Self.

When you are ready and willing to have your blocks revealed to your conscious mind, the information will be presented to you by your Intuitive Self (as it is no longer blocked by the Ego mind) with exactly the right timing so that you are able to cope with confronting the unhelpful beliefs and values that you have stored within. This is the recipe to shining the spotlight on your blocks.

When the Parent voice gets told to take a back seat by the Adult voice, you are on your way. The Child learns it will be heard and no longer needs to sabotage you to get its needs acknowledged and met. Remember always, the Child voice is an inherent part of your personality and it is important to listen to this voice and accommodate its desires, with the help of the Adult and Intuitive Self.

Up until now who has been your decision maker?

So now you need to examine who has been your decision maker. You may have one voice dominate or your voices could be balanced one moment, only to become unbalanced as soon as confrontation appears. We have different coping mechanisms with different situations and stresses. What causes stress to one person may not affect another. Remember your decision maker may shift from Child to Parent to Adult at anytime, depending on your circumstances and what you are dealing with.

Does your Parent run the show most of the time?

If your Parent voice runs the show based on fear, your growth may be thwarted on a regular basis. If you have a nurturing Parent, then as you move forward you will be comforted by self love and support. However, if your Parent overrides the decisions of the Child and Adult you will struggle with the desires of the Child and the Adult not being present. The Child will often sabotage the Parent's control in some manner, or becomes so suppressed that depression sets in to disable the controlling Parent. (See Figure 11)

Your Blocks

Figure 11

Is your Child getting its own way without any restraint?

Without a doubt we all let the Child have its way occasionally, but some people are overrun by their Child. Is your Child demanding and pushy and lacking regard for the consequences in life? Are you taking drugs to your detriment? Are you drinking alcohol to an extent where you are in danger of losing your family or finances? Are you engaging in dangerous acts or behaviours that are putting your life, health or well being at risk? If you answer yes, you probably have your Child running your life. I bet you can hear the criticisms of the Parent, but the Child is stronger and the Adult voice may be non-existent at times. Depending on your conditioning you will have variable responses to these voices. When in pain, often the Parent gives up because it feels unloved, unsupported and insufficient. This sadness that is felt is because the Parent feels like it has lost control, and there is no Adult present for support to make logical decisions. The Parent has become paralysed and the Adult disabled.

Figure 12

Are your Child and Parent constantly fighting for first place?

Ever felt like you couldn't come to a decision because logically or strategically the only possible decisions felt like they didn't really fit or you couldn't be sure of them? This is typical of the Child versus Parent scenario in your mind. This is guaranteed to produce a win-lose situation when the Adult doesn't mediate between the two. When the Adult is not present, either the Child or the Parent wins,

Your Blocks

depending on which voice is stronger. They never both win when the Adult is inactive

Thinking of moving house because you are no longer happy but can't justify the expense and headache of moving? If your Parent wins, you get saddened by being stuck, but if your Child wins you may be at risk of financial hardship.

I think we are all in this position or inner conflict many times throughout our lives when making big decisions. But seriously, the request from the Child comes because you need to grow. The stagnation comes from the Parent because of fear and the need for security and safety based on its conditioning.

If this is your constant contention, then instructions from your Intuitive Self can quickly move you from this level of inner conflict into your Adult voice, which will mediate and allow you to take your best step forward. Learning to listen to your Intuitive Self is covered in Chapter 8.

Figure 13

Mind Chatter That Matters

Is your Adult working toward a win-win for both the Child and Parent?

If you have balance between your Child, Adult and Parent then your discontentment will probably not occur for long. When life throws difficult situations and decisions at you, your Adult can meditate quickly between your Child and Parent, placing limits on your Child and taking into consideration the fears of the Parent. The Child's desires help you grow and the Parent's fears make you aware of your past experiences. However your Adult keeps your hands on the steering wheel of your life.

Figure 14

When we become aware of our thoughts we have the opportunity to become what we choose to think.

Your Blocks

Always keep in mind how the Parent wants a definitive guarantee in order to move forward, as it is driven by its needs of security and safety. The Parent wants a perfected picture of your future, otherwise it shall not participate in growing or obtaining anything new in your life, constantly struggling against change and finding every reason why you cannot grow away from is past conditioning. When the Adult can see how the Parent is driving the decisions based on this conditioning, the Adult can reassure the Parent of the projected future.

Constant forgiveness should be part of your life's purpose in order for your Parent to prevent you from referencing your past hurts and outcomes as ammunition against you for your growth.

Forgiveness is imperative to allow you to release another person who has wronged or hurt you. Forgiveness doesn't mean the other person should not be accountable for their misgivings, it just means that you no longer need to attach to them because they have not been everything you expected them to be. Forgiveness releases you from them; it doesn't release them from their misgivings or mistreatment. You can read more on forgiveness in Chapter 9.

Mind Chatter That Matters

- Chapter 7 -

DIGGING UP YOUR TRASH & TREASURE

In order to analyse the trash and treasures of your life's experience which have been stored in your unconscious mind, you need to give yourself the gift of patience, and not judge yourself too harshly. As you begin to pay attention to your internal voices, you will soon be able to differentiate between the Child, Parent and the Adult voices, particularly when they are in conflict with each other.

Understanding the roles of each of these voices will be of great benefit, and if you feel you need to revisit the earlier chapters, do it now. However, I should point out that even when you are completely one hundred percent comfortable with the intention of each voice, such definitions can still be difficult to deal with.

Remember memories can be recalled from the preconscious mind quite easily. This is where experiences are stored, like the smell of the home cooked apple pie your grandmother used to make, which you can remember without having to think.

The stored experiences which are difficult to recall reside deep within your unconscious mind, and, as such, are difficult to analyse in the present. Therefore, analysing your past decisions and behaviours will result in you reviewing the decisions and actions that were driven by your Child, Parent or Adult in a win-lose, or win-win situation. And yet, simply analysing these will not make a world of difference, as I will explain shortly.

You are not a total sum of your thoughts or experiences

Everything we experience is compiled within the mind to help us make decisions which will hopefully bring about positive life results in the future. Although people endure many negative experiences, they can bury their life experience without even being aware of what has been stored, and whether it is helpful to their life or not. We all unconsciously respond to situations from our experiences and belief systems, which are stored to help back up our defences.

Whilst trying to scrutinise your stored unconscious beliefs and values, remember you are not the total sum of your thoughts and experiences. Thoughts are simply a tool used to expose your experiences, and to help you make decisions. You are a separate

Digging up your Trash & Treasure

being to those thoughts, and all the things which have happened to you. Just because hardship on some level has happened, that doesn't mean hardship is your life, nor does it mean you have to keep responding from this place.

Can you feel you are more than your thoughts? Can you feel that you are more than your body? Can you feel you are more than your experiences, that these experiences were things which happened to you, but are not you? Even if painful, they are still just events. Painful events are no different than the happy events you experienced. You encounter both happy and unhappy events, but they are not you.

You need to question how you have defined your thoughts. Do you define them by:
- what you were told about yourself and the world?
- what you were led to believe?
- what you do?
- how you look?
- your role in life?

Question also how you internalised these experiences. Consider your:
- Parent voice – is it critical, controlling, nurturing, or non-existent?
- Adult voice – is it in control of decisions, or non-existent?
- Child voice – it is overbearing, demanding, too needy, or shut down by the Parent?

In the past, who has been the general winner with your Inner Conflict?

Mind Chatter That Matters

What are your defences?
Are they working for you?
Are you judging others, making them wrong all the time?
Are you on overdrive with self-criticism?
Are you helping, or hindering yourself?
Have you experienced negative life events which you dearly cling to?
Are you acting like a victim to your history, or current circumstances?
Are you clearly making progress in the direction you want?
Are you moving forward, or holding on for dear life, to all you have left?
When breaking up with someone, or having an argument with your partner, are you desperate to win, even if it means losing someone you love?
Are you drinking, or taking drugs, to avoid the pain of what you believe about yourself?

You need to look at your life experiences and the beliefs you have stored, in order to see what is working, and what isn't. Do not let your mind tell you it doesn't matter. Don't stick your head back in the sand, and ignore your unhelpful unconscious belief system. Dig up your trash now, and start examining your past behaviours.

It's time to look at what has been stored in your mind. This book is about changing those beliefs, and using your Intuitive Self to move beyond the pain, and the lousy life you may be living.

If your storage has been unhelpful and your Child or Parent are in control, then have faith, you can gain control over either of these dominating voices.

Digging up your Trash & Treasure

When digging up your Trash and Treasures, make sure you write them down to ensure you can see how other people, outside of your control, have fed you information which was either helpful and loving, or unhelpful to you as an individual. Either way, although it wasn't your fault, it is now **your** responsibility.

A question for you. Who has been your most dominant voice: the Child, or Parent? Most people have one, or the other. Which voice has dominated the most important decisions in your life?

> *The secret to change is to become consciously aware of the choices that your unconscious behaviours drive.*

If your Child is on a self-destructive path to obtain everything it wants, or needs to feel validated, then more than likely your Child wins, and the Parent loses. If your Parent governs every single decision with criticism and control, then more than likely your Parent wins and the Child loses. Often when a Child and Parent are in combat it can take an incredible amount of psychic energy for the Adult to resolve the inner conflict and avoid the situation of there being a winner and a loser.

You need to question whether the beliefs you have stored are really true for you now. If you grew up with beliefs of financial lack, does having a little money now truly suit you as an adult? Does living a loveless life mean your experiences have led you to believe you are now unlovable, when everyone deserves a loving relationship?

Mind Chatter That Matters

How do your beliefs work for you? What beliefs have you changed since your first experiences? If you once believed you were lovable in your teen years but no longer do, then what experience have you had to make you believe you now are no longer worthy of a healthy relationship? How did you gain the clarification to prove you are worthy of a better career? What references have you got that indicate you have changed your beliefs?

Take accountability and ownership for the experiences stored in your unconscious mind, even if someone else contributed to those experiences. Blaming someone else will not help you. They are now your beliefs to own. Own them, and decide if they no longer fit you.

I am sure you have forged new beliefs throughout your entire lifetime, through experiences ranging from growing up in school, learning new maths and spelling words, through to finishing a university degree, or becoming a parent. We all store new information regularly, but it is the persistent unhelpful storage which needs a big shove out of your life, if it isn't working for you.

If you decided a belief was once true, you can now decide if it is no longer true for you.

Although you may have an overnight success in shifting a belief or value, working through your beliefs can be a lifelong work-in-progress. Unravelling old reference points, experiences, beliefs and values is one of the secrets to unlocking your pain, and moving forward with the directives from the Intuitive Self.

Do not be fooled by your Parent's clever guise

Your Parent is very clever at disguising its fear-based agenda. Be aware of the following personality traits, either within yourself as your inner voice or outwardly as your behaviours traits, as they indicate that the Parent is driving the decisions. You will also see these traits in many others around you. When operating from your Intuitive Self, these traits can be overridden with new unconscious beliefs, making you feel happier to make decisions that carry you down a purpose-filled life path.

Ego based around Loss

When your Parent is terrified that it will lose control or its identity, personality traits will appear negatively. Negative fears are based around loss, as the Parent fears that some form of comfort zone is going to be breached, regardless of whether it is good for you or not.

Are you experiencing any of these things inwardly or outwardly?
- Strong desires
- Feeling or being judgemental
- Being critical
- A need to control
- Self fulfilment
- Feeling separate from everyone else
- Self sabotage
- Avoidance of responsibility and/or accountability
- Doubt

Mind Chatter That Matters

- Distrust
- Aloneness
- Lack of support
- Feeling like a victim
- Insecurity
- Blame and powerlessness

Ego based around Gain

Your Parent can be quite sneaky in regards to portraying the ultra confident mask to the outside world and even to you. Sometimes we are not even aware of it. This can be often labelled as "egotistical" when we see this trait in others. When your Parent is terrified that it needs a certain persona for identity, personality traits will appear positively. Positive fears based around gain mean the Parent is in fear, avoiding pain regardless of whether it is going to hold you back.

Inwardly or outwardly, do any of these descriptions apply to you?
- Determined without regard
- Persistently pushy
- Greedy
- Controlling of the outcome
- Limitless
- Arrogant
- Independent from everyone else
- Ignorant to outcome
- Boisterous
- Flamboyant
- Extravagant

Digging up your Trash & Treasure

- Over-social
- Obnoxious
- Overconfident
- Egocentric
- Outwardly secure

It is imperative to review your thinking and behaviour so that you can use your conscious mind to be constantly aware of which voice is making your decision. When your style of thinking is becoming loss or gained-based, you need to consult your Intuitive Self for the right guidance.

Reprogramming your storage

You can obtain some help with reprogramming unhelpful storage in your unconscious mind through many different methods, such as:

- Meditation
- Hypnotherapy
- Kinesiology
- Subliminal messages
- Positive Affirmations
- Self-Talk and Questioning
- Following instructions from your Intuitive Self

Meditation

Practicing meditation is a very good method to help you to live in the present moment, that is, in the conscious mind. When you

Mind Chatter That Matters

first try to meditate you will convince yourself you cannot quieten your mind. You become acutely aware of how busy your mind truly is, and how many thoughts are processed incessantly through it. However, meditation allows you to learn to quieten the mind, and therefore observe your thoughts. It is an excellent technique for becoming aware of what you are thinking. By learning to let go in the moment, it is possible to achieve some peacefulness, even with your thoughts coming and going. Most people experience this Mind Chatter whilst trying to meditate. Persistence with meditation will teach you to put aside your Mind Chatter and feel more whole.

I learnt to meditate in my early twenties, after going through a lot of troubled times in my life. It gave me a sense of peace, where I could observe the fear-based Mind Chatter, and feel connected to something more than I was. I have had many wonderful and informative experiences within my meditative sessions. I strongly recommend you begin and persist with this practice, as it is something you can do in your own home, and even in your car!

Go to my website to find simple free meditation downloads, together with information on the health benefits, and scientific studies.

Hypnotherapy

Hypnotherapy is a form of psychology that can reprogram old beliefs and values, which are stored in your unconscious mind. However, you first need to understand what needs to be changed! Hypnotherapy is only effective if you give permission for these thoughts to be changed. It can also be a useful tool to help recall experiences from the unconscious mind, and therefore can be used to treat patients with various issues from smoking, to anxiety, and subclinical depression.

Kinesiology

Otherwise known as Human Kinetics. Kinesiology studies human and animal movement and performance, and functions with the sciences of biomechanics, physiology, psychology, neuroscience, and anatomy. It is a holistic health discipline, which includes the use of the gentle art of muscle monitoring to access information about a person's emotional, mental, and spiritual well-being.

It is very helpful in finding what experiences and beliefs you have stored in your body, by detecting energy. You will gain a much better understanding on how your mind/body stores energy, and other issues you may not be consciously aware of, which reside in your unconscious mind. I personally have gained tremendous knowledge from this practice, as have the clients I have referred to a Kinesiologist, and I highly recommend you try it at least once to open your mind and heal.

Subliminal messages

Subliminal data suggestions work below the threshold of the conscious mind, by visual or audio stimuli. These generally provide you with suggestions to your unconscious mind. They are similar to hypnotherapy and can be used in conjunction with it.

Mind Chatter That Matters

Positive Affirmations

Many authors, in particular Louise Hay, Dr. Wayne Dyer, Anthony Robbins and Napoleon Hill, believe positive affirmations, or statements of thoughts which the conscious mind hears and processes, will eventually be accepted and become a new belief system for you. I personally have had success with affirmations.

However, some psychologists believe positive affirmations are not effective, leaving people berating themselves when the affirmation didn't work correctly, which results in further negative thoughts and beliefs. They claim affirmations don't work because they target the conscious mind rather than the unconscious mind, and therefore can be incongruent with your beliefs. This can lead to the unconscious mind fighting even harder to hold on to an ingrained belief. Furthermore, they claim declarative self-talk — making self statements of positive (i.e. affirmations) or negative (i.e. core beliefs) — are not as effective as interrogative self-talk.

Self-Talk and Questioning

As mentioned earlier in this chapter, asking yourself is far more powerful than telling yourself something, when you wish to create successful end results. Interrogative analysis and questioning is the first step in reviewing your stored beliefs and values, to evaluate their effectiveness with respect to your current life and goals.

Writing down what you analyse is pertinent to being able to review it later, as it can be difficult to review when your ego mind is attempting

Digging up your Trash & Treasure

to prevent change, and a block can appear if you are trying to sort it all out in your conscious mind. So write, write, write.

Once you have analysed and questioned your ingrained beliefs and values, affirmations used consistently can work for you to override the unconscious. These conscious repetitions will eventually replace the unconscious beliefs stored in your unconscious mind as a result of your past experiences. This method has worked for me and for many others.

You can analyse the hell out of your behaviours, actions, beliefs and values, and get nowhere. Action is needed to bring you results. That is, an action different from what you have done previously.

Every action has an equal reaction

How do you find which action to take when your voices are in conflict and all appear to have valid reasoning? How do you know which voice to follow? You follow the instructions provided to you by your Intuitive Self.

Following instructions from your Intuitive Self

In the following chapter I explain how you can listen to your Intuitive Self, which communicates with your Adult, to give you the guiding light of growth and well-being. You will learn how the Intuitive Self operates, communicates, and supports you for every decision you will ever need to make.

Take a moment to review how many times you overruled your inner gut feeling when making a decision, only to find out later you were totally right. Did you beat yourself up later for not paying attention? Your Intuitive Self will give you all the guidance you need to grow and move forward, even when faced with fear of change, when your mind is in conflict. When you learn how to discern how your Intuitive Self sounds, feels and operates, you will have all the tools you need to live a happy life, regardless of any situation you may encounter, or unhelpful belief system you have stored.

How we beat ourselves up during Inner Conflict

As previously explained, inner conflict is typically your Parent and Child engaged in a constant battle, each struggling to win, and make the other lose. The Parent will create fear through negative self-talk, in order to not move forward and grow. The Parent can be disguised as a self-regulating hand-brake. But when this Parent voice is trying to win, you need to look at its agenda. Is it one of fear, or self-condemnation? Is it holding you back because of its past experiences? Don't allow your Parent to beat you up further for not making a decision the way it wants! When you follow the instructions from your Intuitive Self, the Parent will temporarily take a back seat. However it will still rant on, in the background, with fears. When you have had previous bad decisions or references to experiences, the Parent will use them trying to govern or gain control against the Intuitive Self, Adult and Child.

Digging up your Trash & Treasure

Even if the Child is trying to win the inner conflict, still don't allow the Parent to berate. When the Child wins in the decision making process, no one wins, because it is often an untamed result which can wreak havoc in your life.

Fears – real or imagined?

Are the Parent's fears real, or imagined? As you move forward the Parent will present to you every way in which you can fail. You will feel anxiety, if you keep pushing to grow. Learning to live with anxiety whilst growing is positive, and is healthy to experience. It just doesn't feel like it when you are trying to get your breakthrough.

So what is a fear? A fear is a projected vision of something which hasn't yet occurred. Is it real? No, it isn't. So when you feel fear, or anxiety, push through it, and use your Intuitive Self to guide you. In the next chapter you will learn how your Intuitive Self is there to support you.

Uncomfortable comfort zones

Thinking back on your life, I am sure you would certainly remember instances where you have pushed through comfort zones, like starting a new school, or job.

How many new things have you done in your life which made you break through comfort zones?

Mind Chatter That Matters

Write a list of these events you have moved through, and see how you have the skills needed to do this again and again. Which old beliefs, that once held you back, do you no longer have or are no longer attached to?

Once you have compiled your list of events, circle two of the most difficult ones, and review what levels of discomfort you experienced.

Now write a list of anything which is holding you back right now, and making your life miserable. Next to each one, write down what you believe, or feel you should believe. Pay attention to the negative self-talk. What do you feel you should be doing? What are you certain about? What are the things you could do to change in order to move through these barriers now?

Whilst looking at what we would like to bring into our life to grow, or attract, we still try to apply the same thinking which has kept us in the uncomfortable comfort zone we are stuck in.

Could you break out, and challenge this thinking? Review your patterns of thought by considering:

How the mind tries to lead whilst the Intuitive Self guides you to purpose and passion

---

If you want to grow, but are unsure how to start, or where to start, you need to follow your inner guidance system, your Intuitive Self. Following your Intuitive Self may be completely new to you. However, you need to start somewhere.

- CHAPTER 8 -

YOUR INTUITIVE SELF

In Chapter 4, I explained how you are more than your thoughts, emotions, learned roles, stored experiences and conditioning, and that you have an inner self, which I referred to as your Intuitive Self.

You are a unique self who has been born into this world for a purpose, possibly beyond your knowledge, or understanding, at this point in time. My purpose in writing this book is to help you find purpose and passion in your life. To embrace your uniqueness, compared to the world's billions, to live to the fullest, and be happiest you can possibly be!

Mind Chatter That Matters

If you are not spiritually inclined, please continue reading this chapter, and open your mind to a new possibility. Even if you do not believe in life after death, this chapter will help you. You are able to relate to your gut instinct. Know your gut instinct is your inner self or Intuitive Self. Many people call it many names, but your gut instinct, is simply that. A feeling or sense you get. It communicates to you, and you hear it. You may not always act on it, but you certainly do hear it. Even if only once in your life! If you can hear it, you can develop it further, as it is the secret to learning how the Intuitive Self communicates in a more direct manner to the Adult.

Freud theorised the Child (ID) resides in the unconscious mind, out of awareness. In previous chapters I have explained how you can analyse your Child voice and its attempts to bring its needs, wants and desires into your life without regard to the impact on your life. Don't be concerned if you cannot figure out exactly what it is your Child wants, until you learn about your Intuitive Self. When inner conflict occurs between the Child and Parent a win-lose results. Jung asserts the human psyche energy stops flowing, regressing when thwarted, sending you backward with fear and unwholesomeness. When you learn how to embrace your Intuitive Self's voice, your psyche's energy will move forward.

In Jung's theory of the Collective Unconscious, he posits a concept of synchronicity and having connectedness with one another, plus an individuation of the 'Self' which allows us to be individuals, whilst still being connected to one another. This individuation is what I refer to as the Intuitive Self. Jung claimed that when individuation is obtained, it has a holistic healing effect on a person. Using the Intuitive Self to become whole is how individuation can be obtained

Your Intuitive Self

to enable you to feel connected to the whole of the planet, and your purpose in it.

The trick to "finding yourself, your purpose and passions" resides in the communication between your Intuitive Self and your Adult. Your Intuitive Self will show you exactly what your Child needs are, and how to bring them into your life by giving instructions to your Adult on the steps to guide your life's purpose and passions in a safe way. This allows the Adult to embrace the Child voice into its observing and decision making process.

Learning how to pay attention to your Intuitive Self will move you forward in leaps and bounds, and bring incredible happiness and purpose in your life. This chapter will explain what your Intuitive Self is, how it feels and communicates, and how to pay attention to it. In the next chapter, you will learn how to take better care of your inner self on a regular basis, so it can be your *Mind Chatter That Matters* to you.

Depending on what you believe, are reading, learning or listening to, your Intuitive Self voice is called many names, such as:
- Gut feeling, or inner knowing
- Heart sense
- Soul, Spirit, or Higher Self
- Inner Self
- Divine Guidance
- Vibration
- Inner Energy, and so on.

This book is not a debate on whether there is, in fact, a continuation

Mind Chatter That Matters

of life after death of the human race. Cultures all over the world believe in life after death. I am sure you have experienced feeling an internal instruction on some level, which you have perhaps ignored, and later regretted.

How many times have you ignored your inner sense? Did you ignore it when it told you not to drive up a certain road? Did you drive in the direction you thought to be right, only to find your inner sense was correct? Or perhaps there were times when you knew something was going to happen, but tried to think differently, and your inner sense was right again! Or you might have met someone who you sensed was not a good person, and ignored the feeling, only to later receive confirmation you were right all along!

Figure 15

Your Intuitive Self

Time and time again, we ignore this inner sense, or gut feeling, which speaks to us regularly, daily, or hourly. Remember a time when your life looked like it was falling apart, and could not get any worse, then you heard a little voice say "it will be ok"? Everyone has an Intuitive Self; however, we are all guilty of not paying attention to it, even me. Recently, I was booking an airline ticket and sensed I should take the 12 midnight flight. Nevertheless, I wanted to book the 4pm, because I thought it would be a better flight. I debated for a few minutes, went ahead, and booked the 4pm flight, ignoring my Intuitive Self, only to arrive five minutes late for the 4pm flight. Guess what flight I was on next? Yes, the 12 midnight. I was perched in the airport for another 8 hours, waiting for the flight I had sensed I should take in the first place.

Over time we learn to listen to the messages we get from our Intuitive Self, learning how accurate it is in providing messages of guidance.

Your Intuitive Self's purpose

Your Intuitive Self has one major purpose in your life, which is to guide you in a positive and helpful direction, and to enable you to grow as a person. It is a supportive source of love and honour to you, and it is wise to take its counsel seriously. This counsel will encourage you to grow and develop to your maximum potential, providing endless opportunities for positive growth and learning. It will help you find your true nature, which is independent of how you have been conditioned, what your Tribe has led you to believe, or your life experiences. It is a part of a bigger consciousness.

Mind Chatter That Matters

When embraced fully, you will discover a whole new side to your personality, one which is confident and trusting and can deal with life's ups and downs, or other people's lack of love and support.

Decision making becomes simple when you can hear your Intuitive Self's voice giving clear instructions. Internal conflict becomes a thing of the past, or only occupies your mind for small moments of time, until you recognise the Parent vs. Child battle occurring.

During difficult and trying times in your life, listening to this inner guidance will show you exactly what you need to do next. It will guide you to self-support using emotional intelligence, rather than needing to depend on other people for long periods.

Loving others becomes something you offer without conditions. Giving love will no longer be something you do in order to receive love in return.

Punishment is never on the Intuitive Self's agenda, as it is forgiving and disciplined, dealing with only current issues and giving unconditional loving guidance, regardless of the mishaps and misdemeanours in the present, or past. This in turn also brings about self-forgiveness, as you internalise its presence.

Your Intuitive Self will help you heal from painful experiences and hurts, learning from these experiences rather than being victims of them.

You will become disentangled from distorted emotions, and move toward the natural emotions, which are positive and uplifting.

Your Intuitive Self

Your feelings of emptiness and worthlessness will subside and you will begin to fill your void, because you sense a loving support within, as things start to change for the better in your life. You become less needy of people, material things, or money, and see them as a pleasure to have in your life, rather needing them to feel important or worthy.

You will learn a sense of equality with other people as you learn to accept your differences, and to understand everyone has their own purpose. No one is right or wrong, as each individual is having their own life experience, and we are in different life classrooms, with different learning abilities.

Respect for yourself becomes a gift you exude without the need to induce fear in other people in order to try to gain respect or trust. People naturally respect others who have this presence about them.

Your life path will be shown to you with step by step instructions towards your purpose. This brings the passion into your life by allowing you to live your life authentically with your own values, rather than those you were conditioned with. The Parent's storage of unconscious beliefs and values is challenged, and fear arises, but your Intuitive Self has the tools and confidence to deal with these fears.

Everyone has their own Intuitive Self; it is our gift at birth, together with our instinctual drive to survive. Even if you cannot feel or sense this gift, you can learn to.

Mind Chatter That Matters

How the Intuitive Self communicates to you

The Intuitive Self will communicate in several different ways: visions, thoughts, dreams, hunches, gut feelings, pictures, video clips, music, ideas, designs, creations, warnings, support messages, knowingness etc. will just pop into your awareness randomly, without you thinking about them.

As I explain to my clients and course attendees, you can tell the difference between your thoughts, and those of your Intuitive Self, by the way your brain processes the information. For example, when you are thinking, speaking or listening to someone, pay attention, as the words are repeated in your head in order for you to absorb this information. That's your brain processing the information. When speaking, you are asking, or making statements in your mind, but there is processing. When reading, it's like you are repeating the words on the page, and then your brain processes the information you have read. When listening it's the same; you literally repeat what someone is saying. It happens in a split second. You are present, aware, and absorbing the information. As your brain sifts through, it aligns the information with your beliefs and values, choosing to accept, or reject the information according to your stored experiences and knowledge. The difference between your own brain processing, and your Intuitive Self, is that there is no processing in the latter case where your thoughts, images, dreams, or gut feelings just randomly turn up. They seem to appear from nowhere. They are very random, and often occur when you are not thinking about an issue or solution, nor consciously aware or in the present moment. A thought or image will often be presented to you by your Intuitive

Your Intuitive Self

Self while you are in the middle of doing something totally unrelated to the information given.

This may be a little confusing at first, and if you are not sure just recollect if you had some form of processing going on beforehand. This is how to tell the difference between your thoughts and the voice of your Intuitive Self.

Have you ever noticed bells ringing, or red flags about a person, and you totally ignored it, only to be hurt, or deceived by that person at a later stage? Ever got the gut feeling something was wrong with someone, then later found out they have a terminal illness? I'm sure you have put food in your mouth knowing it is not good for your health, but went ahead anyway, only to later find you have an intolerance to such food. Do you feel like your relationship is past its used by date, but your mind is still holding on? Ever sensed a downturn in the business and felt it was time to move on from a job, but you stayed because of financial security, only to be retrenched later? Are your fears holding you back even though you feel one hundred percent driven? These are examples of how we don't pay attention to our Intuitive Self's voice; we allow our Parent or Child to drive the decisions of our life, only to find out later that the Intuitive Self was right in the first instance. The more you pay attention to your Intuitive Self, the happier you will become. Your Intuitive Self will provide the right guidance for you to get in touch with your life's passions and purpose. Living by, and honouring your Intuitive Self will certainly bring the sense of wholeness which Carl Jung has clearly documented.

Please note: the Intuitive Self will only ever show you messages which will move you forward, and are positive, loving, supportive, and uplifting. They are never messages to harm yourself, or anyone else. If you are having any thoughts of harming yourself, or anyone else, please seek professional help immediately.

Becoming open to your Intuitive Self

To be able to pay attention to your Intuitive Self, you must first will it. What I mean by this, is be prepared to hear your Intuitive Self, give it way, open yourself to the possibility it will help you. You must trust that you have all the tools within you to deal with your life's journey and learning. You will become more conscious of this inner voice which resides within you, a voice that that you may have hardly, or never, paid attention to.

When you start to become aware of these messages from your Intuitive Self they may not always seem to make sense. Often, when you first begin to pay attention, these messages appear like bits of a puzzle. Firstly, just pay attention, the puzzle pieces will all appear. Store the memory of the puzzle pieces, and they will fall into place. When you are ready to move forward (not in your ego mind but on a soul level) the final puzzle piece will fall into place to provide a clear picture of your direction. I am sure you have had this experience with different endeavours in your life.

Often when the Intuitive Self is becoming more present in your life you may feel like you have no direction and are confused about the future, feeling lost and disorientated. You may find yourself feeling like you can no longer relate to some of the people who have been

Your Intuitive Self

around you of late, and you feel very different, or as if you need a change of environment. Ego centred people seem to irritate you more than ever. Money, or material things, have lost their lustre, or importance, to your happiness. Nothing you do seems to fit, or seems pointless, or fruitless (not in a depressive way). You may feel like the old you no longer fits who you are, but you have no idea of what you are to become. You no longer feel the need to please everyone else, but are not sure how to start pleasing you. You are sure you cannot keep going in the direction you have been, but keep thinking of ways to make your direction clearer, only to feel more confused and unsettled. You will feel like no one truly understands your dilemma, and you are on your own with forging a new path. Your mind chatter will probably be at a peak level, trying to sort out a new direction, and a new you.

This is when the Intuitive Self will attempt to show you guidance, to assist you with your lack of direction. It will show you your way out, if you can find the courage to honour it and follow its directions. You will hear messages of direction which will flare your fears to a whole new height, because your Intuitive Self will help you to push through the Parent's agenda and the comfort zones that exist because of the conditioning of your unconscious mind. Fear is perfectly normal during the process of following the guidance of your Intuitive Self. Learning to work through fear is a reward for following the Intuitive Self's guidance. To expand your comfort zone is to learn new ways of doing things which will later reinforce new conditioning into your unconscious mind, making you feel more secure and whole in yourself.

Your Intuitive Self will give very direct and clear statements to you.

Mind Chatter That Matters

It doesn't mince words. Any blocks in your understanding will be your Parent blocking this information, because of its fear of change or acknowledging fault. Your Adult has all the tools to use the guidance given to make clear and decisive actions. You will learn to put your Parent back in its place, to have a role of nurturing support, rather than controlling you by critical, guilt inducing submission.

If you are experiencing fear of change, celebrate! This is a good thing. Become aware of the need to change, acknowledge your fears, but forge ahead anyway, regardless of the overruling Parent's condemnation.

Trusting your Intuitive Self voice

As you begin to follow guidance shown to you by your Intuitive Self, and see the positive results in your life, pat yourself on the back. You deserve it. Great work. You may not change overnight, suddenly following every instruction, or guidance shown to you. It takes time to learn to recognise the guidance, and each person grows at a different rate. Sometimes you may take two steps forward, and one back. As long as you are growing, no one is measuring your pace. You are not accountable to anyone but yourself, even if you have been conditioned to believe you have to answer to someone.

Learning to trust your innate guidance system means to follow the deep knowing or feeling you have. Do not let your controlling Parent con you into following its guise. Your Intuitive Self voice is assertive, empathic and unambiguous, and makes clear and simple statements of guidance to you in a gentle, soft or quiet, loving tone.

Your Intuitive Self

By contrast, the Parent voice is loud and aggressive, controlling, coercive, and very fearful of change. You will learn to recognise the Parent, and its agenda; you will learn how to override this aspect of your mind, to fully embrace the guidance from your Intuitive Self. Using your Adult to make the decisions with the guidance from your Intuitive Self will allow you the freedom to sit with your fears, shutting down the Parent's negative aspect, and allowing your Child freedom of expression.

As you begin to implement more of the guidance from your Intuitive Self you will begin to feel excited, positive, and uplifted with a bright hope for your future. Bundled together with this will be trepidation, anxiety, apprehension or fear about moving away from your comfort zone. Very rarely will your Child be active at this stage, because the Intuitive Self is taking care of implementing the Child's needs, wants and desires. Freud maintains the Child (ID) lies in your unconscious mind, but I believe your Intuitive Self has the ability to gently bring the needs of your Child (which are the purpose of your life) forward, into your conscious mind.

When the Child is getting its needs and wants taken care of, the Parent is being conditioned to new experiences, and the Adult is supporting the entire process with the guidance of the Intuitive Self, the true happiness and wholeness Jung described can be obtained.

In confronting the fears of the Parent you become more confident of your Intuitive Self's guidance. An inner self-confidence grows from forging ahead.

Working through this process, time and time again, allows your

Mind Chatter That Matters

unconscious mind to be updated with new reference points and experiences. Your conditioning becomes more whole, and allows you to self-love and support; you no longer need to reach outside of yourself for love and support, as you had been conditioned to do.

Love is a gift when given, but to expect love can be disappointing. People's circumstances constantly change, and they can easily change their minds about how much time, or energy they have to offer. Learning how to love and support yourself using your Intuitive Self is very rewarding, as when other people cannot fill up your void, you begin to fill it yourself. You find you, and you feel more whole because you no longer need to depend on people or possessions to make you feel better.

If the voice of the Intuitive Self is no longer suppressed, you can begin to embrace the guidance, and your mind chatter begins to quieten as your unconscious beliefs are updated with new reference points which are positive, and self-sufficient. When you follow the positive moves to grow you are automatically rewarded, because you feel aligned with you, not the rest of the world, or your Tribe. Your Parent voice becomes more loving and nurturing toward you, no longer needing to control the outcome, because the negative experience and conditioning has been overwritten with new positive beliefs and values. You begin to value you. This is individuation.

Your Mind Chatter will no longer be regularly in conflict. Even when you have negative issues to deal with, you trust you have the skills to deal with them, regardless of their degree of difficulty. You may slip back into some old patterns, those which haven't been overwritten yet, but you become aware faster, and quickly correct your decision

Your Intuitive Self

making process.

The ego mind pushes, whilst the Intuitive Self guides. This is the fundamental difference! Your ego mind will want a guarantee in writing, signed, sealed, and delivered. It wants proof the impossible can be made possible, and believes something is achievable only after it has become real. The Intuitive Self, on the other hand, knows that it can be achieved, that you can make it real. In other words, the mind wants it real first, before believing, while the Intuitive Self makes it real by believing in it.

You are a creative being

Humans are creative beings. Everything other than true nature, every material thing, is manufactured by man. Someone designed a product that didn't seem impossible, and saw it through to the manufacturing stage so that other people could enjoy the fruits of one person's creative thinking. The creator followed his or her Intuitive Self until the creation became real.

When creators create, they believe something is possible which has not yet been achieved. They will commit many hours, weeks, and even years to the development. From sewing a new dress, to manufacturing the latest high tech gadget, this creation process occurs daily, and is no different to creating the life we want.

When you believe you can buy a new car, it doesn't just turn up in the driveway, does it? You think about getting a new car, how it looks, the model, how you are going to pay for it, and go out searching for

Mind Chatter That Matters

the one you want. Then, presto, it turns up in your driveway. You created this car in the driveway using your thoughts, together with your actions, to make it happen.

This process is no different to wanting to attract a new mate into your life, when you are truly ready. You decide on the type of person you want, and start to prepare yourself for a new relationship. Then, by some strange coincidence, a new relationship happens. Your thoughts attracted another person who was looking as well.

This creative process begins in the mind. The Law of Attraction is a certainty in my world, and I know it can be in yours. Take a moment to recollect all the negative things you have thought about and attracted, along with the positive things you have attracted. Awareness of the Law of Attraction will shed some light on why many people attract the same type of relationship over and over again. This is because they are attracting according to their unconscious experiences, and conditioning, which are governing their thoughts and mind.

If you feel stuck, and can see how you repeat the same mistakes, or patterns over and over, you need different thoughts and actions.

The definition of insanity is doing the same things over and over and expecting a different result

---

Dig up your trash from your unconscious mind, and analyse it.

Your Intuitive Self

Next follow the guidance your Intuitive Self as to what you need to change, so you can bring happiness into your life.

Choosing the voice that wins

If you pay attention and follow the guidance of your Intuitive Self, your life will flow much better and opportunities will arrive out of nowhere. Things seem to fall into place, people turn up to help you at the right time, because you are being guided by an innate system which just simply works. As Carl Jung described it, synchronicity is where the collective unconscious works with you with ease.

YOU have the POWER to CREATE the LIFE you WANT!

Generally, if you are not paying much attention to the Intuitive Self, then you will feel stuck. Things do not flow, relationships can be difficult and trying. Life can be a struggle, and can appear negative.

We often attempt to make logical decisions based on fairly logical reasoning. However, if your Intuitive Self is guiding you in a different direction, follow your Intuitive Self. There will certainly be a reason for it.

Making the choice over which voice rules the decision making is a sensible approach to your Mind Chatter, as soon as you become aware of the voices, and their driving force, and wants. Getting to know your Intuitive Self and how reliable it is for you will take time, and while you are learning to trust in it fully you will probably make some mistakes. Forgive yourself, because you are learning.

Mind Chatter That Matters

When you don't pay attention to your Intuitive Self, the message is simply repeated in the same manner, or in a different one, until you pay attention. Its volume doesn't increase, or become more aggressive, it just simply is what it is, a small quiet voice waiting for your awareness.

However, if you don't pay attention to the Parent or Child voices, they will become louder, aggressive, and more overbearing even than before. Fear will be rampant, and anxiety levels will peak. This is the Parent's method of control, to stay fixed, and unchanged. The Child will do things to sabotage you when it is not heard.

Become aware of these tactics, try to listen to your Intuitive Self, and you will find your individual answers to unblocking your life, and understanding your mind chatter.

If you are unable to sense the guidance from your Intuitive Self, try these things:
- Sit quietly, and let your thoughts drift, or meditate for peacefulness
- Ask your Intuitive Self (or what name you call it) for guidance to show you the direction you need
- Sit with yourself for a few minutes appreciating the good in you
- Feel a sense of gratitude for what you do have in your life now
- Don't think about the solution to your conflict, feel it
- Pray, if you are so inclined, and ask for assistance
- Your answers will appear, but not necessarily instantly.

Your Intuitive Self

How can you integrate?

Use your conscious mind to observe your four voices.

With every inner conflict or indecision, check figure 16 below to ascertain which voice is giving you information, and then analyse that information. Using the information given throughout this book you should be able to see each voice's agenda. This is a good time to write everything down and categorise each piece of information, and then label each point with a voice.

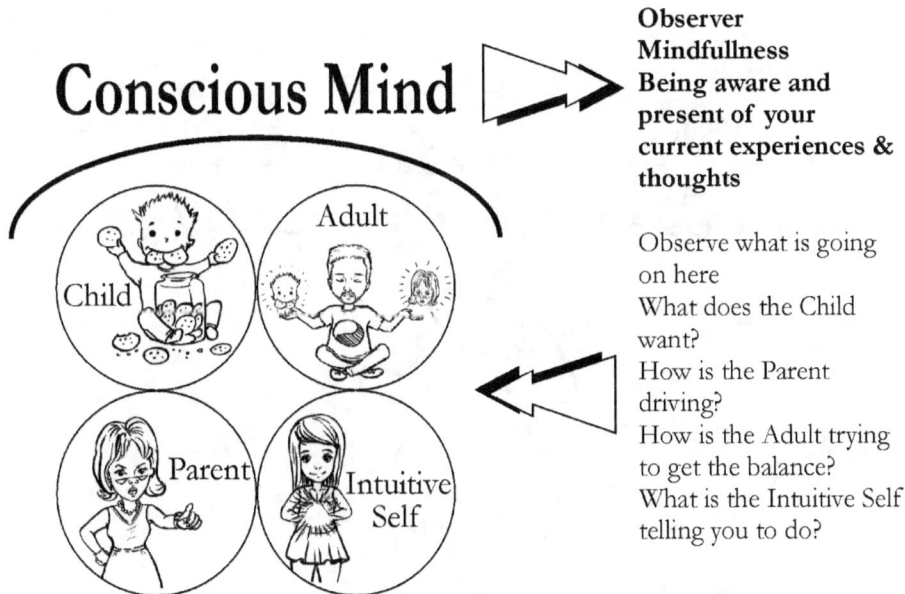

Figure 16

Mind Chatter That Matters

Beginning to be guided by your Intuitive Self can happen in little steps at first. Follow it every now and then and test it if you must. Following your Intuitive Self can at first be very daunting, but think back to a time where you did follow your Intuitive Self or gut instinct and it didn't fail you. One step at a time. Sometimes you will think you are following your Intuitive Self, only to realise that it was your Parent making the decisions again. Be kind to yourself and keep going.

Figure 17

Your Intuitive Self

Light vs. Dark

When your inner conflict begins, refer to Table 1 in Chapter 4, where I touched on natural and distorted emotions to help you confirm what emotions you are experiencing. Are they more distorted, or natural? Inner conflict will often produce distorted emotions, so it is imperative you review your current conflict and see what is holding you back.

I believe the distorted emotions are those of the darker energy of the ego mind, and the natural ones are of light and love, which you can work towards, regardless of how difficult your conflict is.

You are gifted with the ability to choose light or dark, natural or distorted emotions. Make a choice to work towards the light daily, regardless of your troubles.

The Child (ID) is your personality, and your purpose in life, which is shown to you through your Intuitive Self. It is what makes you an individual, separate from everyone else, but yet still connected through the Collective Unconscious. Use your Intuitive Self to bring through your purpose in this life in order to enjoy it, rather than being held back by your conditioning and experiences, hurt and pain, trials and tribulations. Each person on this planet has a purpose, you just may not be aware of it yet. Your purpose could be running a country, being a world humanitarian leader, being a mother, or being a garbage collector. Status is not relative — your contribution to fellow humans, animals and nature is what counts, even if it is emptying bins, as those who do that contribute to the cleanliness of society. Mother Theresa was a simple nun who brought a new understanding and gentleness to the world. You have something to contribute, even if it is being a mum to your beautiful children, who may become global change makers. You are a fundamental piece of the collective unconscious. Be present in your life, and learn to love your purpose. When in tune with your purpose, you will feel passionate about your life, and your uniqueness, no longer needing to be compared to another person. Be proud to be an individual, and never compare yourself to another person's outside persona, or mask.

When you are on the journey of learning to honour your Intuitive Self, you may hide it from others, because they cannot always understand what you are working through, or they possibly may not have an understanding of your new processes. You may even feel like they are a little alien to you now. Please don't push anyone else to grow because you love and treasure them; they will recognise the need for change, and start looking for answers themselves. When they see your growth, and the way you model success and happiness, you will be their first point of contact to find out your recipe for success.

> ***When the student is ready,***
> ***the teacher will appear.***

This type of growth may appear a little different, and may be rejected, or at least not accepted, by logical thinkers. It is not your place to judge, as they are as individual as you, and on their own learning journey. Preaching to someone doesn't work, modelling does. So model your new passionate and purposeful you, as often as you can, forgiving yourself when you slip up. After all, you are only human!

True goal setting

Once you become aware of your Intuitive Self, you will never become unaware. It will always be there. However, you may at times forget to follow it. You will find your hindsight is perfect for showing you where you didn't follow the guidance.

True goal setting will become available to you as you embrace the guidance of your Intuitive Self, as life becomes more about the goals you are meant to obtain to fulfil your purpose, rather than being driven by monetary needs or security. These new goals may be challenging, yet you will be rewarded with growth, learning, confidence, and self-worth.

Mind – body relationship

There are many books worthy of reading on this topic. Even if you don't believe in the relationship between the mind and the body, what you create in your mind, your body will also experience. Your body is a very willing apparatus, following instructions from your brain faster than the speed of light. We take this process completely for granted. Thoughts are no different from the other instructions your body receives from your brain. When you feel joy, you feel energised, and want to jump out of your body. When you feel sadness, you feel de-energised, and you want to rest and be comfortable. Your body will adapt to your thoughts whether they are negative or positive,

Mind Chatter That Matters

regardless of how accurate, truthful, or real they are.

Have you ever been with someone who started laughing, and you had no idea why, but started to laugh at them, or with them? Laughing is happy energy, and it's infectious. If you think happy thoughts, your body will respond to those happy thoughts. The reverse is also true.

When stuck in your controlling Parent, your mind's thinking may also become stuck and unhealthy. Your Intuitive Self will love and support you to better health, as you learn to listen to it.

When you are feeling low you can ascertain your symptoms and go to a doctor for help, but what led you to get sick in the first place? Make sure it is not negative, victimising thoughts from your unconscious mind making you sick. If you feel negativity over your head like a dark cloud, don't be afraid to talk to someone who can professionally help you, because you may eventually fall ill as a result of your thinking.

Many authors have written cancer is a disease from angry thinking, where the body turns on itself, and starts eating away at you. If this is true, internalising anger is certainly bad for your health, let alone your mind. How many other diseases are created with the mind? Although these are theories, I believe they hold a great weight in the Mind-Body connection.

Use the tools in this book to guide you towards better health in your Mind and Body.

Your Intuitive Self

When your Intuitive Self voice is awakening, speaking and guiding you

When the Intuitive Self starts to awaken, or guide you, it seems like you are standing in a thick heavy fog. Everything seems to not work, and is blocked. You may feel disjointed, and you cannot see what you are meant to do, or where you are meant to be. When this occurs your ego mind is attempting to run the decision making process, but you just don't like any of the decisions, or the solutions don't seem to fit. You cannot find a key which fits any doors in life or career, relationships, living arrangements, family, life purpose, and passions. You simply cannot make sense of the heavy fog, and cannot clearly see the path forward. When this situation appears, the fog will not clear until you listen to your Intuitive Self voice. You will sense what you need to do, even though the ego mind is vying for first place in the decision making process. Often the Adult feels frantic as it tries to sort out a decision between the Parent and Child.

The Parent wants to stay put, the Child wants to move forward. The fogginess makes you feel as if you can't make a decision, and it is the ego mind's method of blocking your vision forward, thereby securing its position and having the security of no change. Prior to this fog appearing in your mind, you will often feel a sense of change coming, but you may not have paid much attention to what that change may be. It is common for people to consult either a counsellor or psychic at this point in time in order to gain better clarification of the decision they need to make.

When the fog appears in your mind this is a perfect time to allow the Intuitive Self to guide you, and the path forward shall start to

Mind Chatter That Matters

appear. You will receive guidance in the form of signs. Pay attention to indicators your mind notices, like a new advertisement, name, or random thought, which will lead you to the right place. When you want a new direction in life, it is like wanting a door to open, or to have a peek at what is behind it. However, you will sense the door is tightly locked because the psyche doesn't have the ability to see its path when the Intuitive Self voice is speaking. You need to implement trust at this time, as the Intuitive Self shall never deny you guidance, or teachings, and when you allow this trust, light is shone on your path and you will develop an awareness of what you have to do to move forward after all your inner conflict. The more you practice listening to your Intuitive Self, the more loudly it will speak, and you will pay attention. Then you shall rely on it more, and repeat the process of growing, to know your true inner self, your spirit. Further to this, you will feel your sense of spirit become alive, and you will become acutely aware of when you overruled the Intuitive Self. You'll say, "I knew I shouldn't have done that," or "I should've done this"!

It is not about leaving your destiny to others. It's about following the destiny shown to you by your Intuitive Self

---

Once you learn to Observe, Analyse and Act from your conscious mind, are paying attention to the Mind Chatter That Matters, and begin being guided by your Intuitive Self, you can:
- Learn to sit with your fears, as they are not real, just projections from your Parent
- Use your creative mind to grow and attract what you need

Your Intuitive Self

  in life to be able to embrace your Intuitive Self's guidance
- Ask for what you want from a higher power for the greater good of all
- Trust that you are part of the Collective Unconscious that will take care of your order and contribution to the entire universal system.
- Feel gratitude when you receive what you need, exactly when you need it
- Check that your requests to a higher power do not conflict with one another.
- Appreciate your own innate guidance system over and over again!
- Allow the guidance of the Intuitive Self to be acted upon by your Adult, and keep your Parent at bay. Your Adult has the ability to make the best decisions based on the knowingness of your Intuitive Self, and the Child's passions, and purpose.

To sum up, the Intuitive Self appears in some or all of these ways:
- Gut instinct
- Random thoughts
- Premonitions
- Through dreams
- Unexplained insights
- Knowingness – but not from experience
- Spiritual experiences – seeing or hearing dead people
- An inner gut feeling to do something
- A driving force that is for the greater good
- Having/wanting a connection to the world and all its inhabitants

Mind Chatter That Matters

- Loving others, without conditions
- Acceptance of self and of others' differences
- Words of wisdom
- Psychic experiences of visions, smell or hearings
- Natural gifts and talents that you were not taught previously.

To sum up, these are the signs you are awakening to your Intuitive Self:

- You feel like you are in a thick heavy fog and cannot see your way clear
- Your direction is unknown or cannot be guaranteed by the Parent, and fear is reigning
- You are feeling blocked in that you have no idea who you are anymore
- You feel like you need a new direction or need to grow, but have no idea what that growth looks like
- Confusion when your Parent voice is trying to make the decisions and you know that it isn't right for you to follow
- You have a hunch or sense some sort of change coming but have no idea of what it is
- You see signs of synchronicity that you would like to follow up on, but your Parent is preventing change
- Knowingness that you are about to embark on something but have no idea how to go about it
- Your life seems to no longer fit you and you are ready to embrace change no matter what your Parent is deciding.

And the Intuitive Self will teach you:

- Individuation comes from seeing and accepting your uniqueness

Your Intuitive Self

- That this material world is not all there is
- To believe that there is more to this life
- To feel connected to nature and its purpose
- To grow and develop – not for egotistical reasons
- To recognise your need to have a spiritual connection to a higher power
- To believe that synchronicity is real
- To believe that we are all connected with one another
- To sense your inner and outer 'Self'.

You will sense certain attributes of the Intuitive Self operating within you. When your Intuitive Self starts to speak you will notice:

- A small quiet voice (becoming louder when observed regularly)
- A deep knowing that the message is right
- That you often ignore the small voice until you embrace it
- You feel scared to embrace it, as there appears to be no guarantees for the Parent
- Listening to the Intuitive Self will quieten the Child
- You feel that you are moving away from the fear-based thoughts and behaviour characteristic of the ego mind (ego based around loss or ego based around gain)
- You feel inter-dependence with everyone else
- You become more trusting of the outcome
- You feel fuelled by your own gifts and potential
- You lovingly accept yourself and others
- You know where your passion exists and you can embrace it
- You are aware of your life purpose
- You understand your life experience

Mind Chatter That Matters

- You accept your experiences and lessons
- And, most of all, YOU WILL KNOW when your gut instinct or inner self or soul is speaking!

Know that this Intuitive Self is for your greater good and also for the greater good of all the other habitants of the world, including nature and its wonders.

Staying connected to your inner spirit can essentially enhance your quality of life, both mentally, and physically. Remember spirituality is a dynamic process, and a constantly evolving internal journey. Your personal definition of spirituality may change with your age, and your life experiences. But it will always form the basis of your well-being, help you maintain a reasonable stress level, and affirm your purpose in life.

Some people pray, or ask for assistance from a higher power. They may ask God, Jesus or Allah to give them the results they desire, or need. Praying to receive, without your Intuitive Self's intent, is like asking for a gift without believing that you really deserve it. When you ask from the ego mind for things that are not aligned with your Intuitive Self, no matter how much you pray or ask, the higher power cannot overwrite your will, or your life's passions and purpose or intent of your Intuitive Self and you will not receive what was asked for.

What is not understood is that most people's requests are from the ego mind and such requests for assistance are often to avoid pain or gain pleasure rather than the highest good of you or others and therefore do not activate the Law of Attraction accurately as

Your Intuitive Self

they relinquish your own accountability to obtain what is needed for their life's purpose and passion. When you ask for a solution to your pain or wish to gain pleasure then it will not teach you how to obtain that which you need. Therefore you are not attracting that which is truly required for your growth. Requesting assistance is best asked in the form of "What is it that I am meant to learn or do for this issue."

When you engage your Intuitive Self's intent, or will, then the higher power has the ability to bring you exactly what you need or what you need to learn, thus transforming the energy of your intent into reality in your world.

Scientists have even proven everything is energy in this world; solid matter (wood, metal, glass and living things etc.) is energy that resonates at a lower frequency than other energy forms such as light and heat. Thought is energy too. So, if it is only energy, you can attract what you need to fulfil your true purpose and passions.

When you truly own your request, you need to take action: start making steps and looking for what you need. Your request will simply not drop into your lap because you requested it. Your awareness, responsibility, accountability, and actions demonstrate you are ready for the Law of Attraction to be activated.

Firmly acknowledge the life purposes shown to you by your Intuitive Self, and unconditionally own them. Then ask, or pray for assistance in achieving these purposes, and in conquering any fears which may evolve. The oneness of the universe hears your request, and your commitment to achieving your Intuitive Self's life purpose

Mind Chatter That Matters

and passion. You will be assisted, maybe not directly, but you will be shown the direction, or helped to learn what it is you need to bring what you want into your life.

Further to this, have no expectation on how your request will be attracted to you. It may take several steps. Check in with your Intuitive Self, and take action when guided, as your Intuitive Self knows the direction you need to take in order to receive, and grow into your request.

Asking for healing, or other things, for another person may also be overwriting their will, so when you ask under these circumstances, release the need to control, and give up any expectations of the outcome. This can be incredibly difficult when you love someone who is terminally ill. When we release the need for a specific outcome, and allow the other person their own will, that does not mean you are ever left feeling unloved and unsupported by a higher power. Remember everyone in this world is born with spirit, and will leave as spirit when the time is absolutely perfect for them. This can often leave us feeling bereft, and create misconceptions of the reasons for death, and the way it happens.

I recall in 1995, when my mother fell ill with bowel and liver cancer. I asked her, "I want to ask you Mum, do you truly feel it is your turn to die, or not?" She replied with total honesty, "I know it is my time now." Most people know this, but fight against their inner knowing, because of fear of death and the unknown. My beautiful mother is now one of my guides, helping me help others. You cannot deny the messages which come from the Intuitive Self, but you can ignore them, or not act on them.

Your Intuitive Self

The higher power has no control over you, as you have your own will, that of the ego mind, and that of the Intuitive Self; it is your choice which you follow. Spirit never brings negative events into our lives to teach us lessons. We attract these negative lessons until we learn to follow our Intuitive Self. These negative lessons are triggered by lack of learning, and from our lack of understanding of the ego mind and our failure to embrace our true loving selves. We sacrifice our own innate ability to be happy because we are brainwashed, early in our lives, to believe that our needs are external, when we have everything we need internally, connected to a oneness which is often very misunderstood. However, the higher power will provide for you when you allow your Intuitive Self to show you the path to your true life purpose and passions. This is where true joy is found.

In the next chapter I explain how to better nurture yourself so you can become closer to your Intuitive Self and embrace the true guidance, love and support you have on offer.

Mind Chatter That Matters

- Chapter 9 -

SELF-CARE

You may feel unloved, and bewildered, if you leave your destiny and happiness in the hands of other people, at the mercy of their actions or decisions. When you take care of yourself, in a holistic manner, you become the driver of your life. Self-care is a process which unfolds in a natural way, as you learn to honour and love yourself as no one else can.

Now that you have the tools to learn how to listen to the guidance of your Intuitive Self, there are a few things which will help you to get started, and stay on, your new path of loving, honouring and caring for yourself holistically.

Steps for Self-care

These 22 points are in no particular order, and you may feel not all of them apply to you at a given time.

1. Give yourself permission to be different to everyone else

One of the first steps to self-care is to stop comparing yourself to anyone else. Acceptance of your uniqueness is a must. It doesn't matter how different or eccentric you may be. You are still you. Grant yourself permission to be totally you, and no one else. Being different is fabulous!

2. Give yourself permission to mess up occasionally

There will be times you feel like you take two steps forward, and one back. You think you are moving forward, and all of a sudden you're going backward again, as you realised you didn't pay attention or that you missed something. Don't beat yourself up when you mess up; just make another decision to go forward. As long as you are moving forward, at whatever pace, you are not going in a backward direction. Growth is about learning what works and what doesn't. You are not perfect, no one is.

Self-Care

3. Be flexible

Adopt a flexible approach to reaching your goals of self-care and growth. Accept that your goals, or road map, may change along the way. Your plan, or your vision of your destination, will undoubtedly change. You may have envisioned a straight long journey, but it may move in a zigzag direction. You will be tested, and when things are getting difficult, you are almost at your breakthrough for change. Stick with your road, no matter how you envisioned it, as your journey is one of learning more about yourself.

4. Letting go

As you begin to recognise the many things holding you back from growing, letting go is a loving act to do for yourself. Letting go releases you from the ties binding you to old unhelpful patterns, addictions, people, jobs, money, status, and material things. When you are stuck in your life with something which no longer serves you, give yourself permission to look for another option, and let go of what is not working.

Some people will make your transition more difficult than it should be because they are benefiting from your contribution to their lives, and your growth can make them feel insecure. If they are not wanting, or willing, to allow you to grow occasionally, reassurance is needed for the other person. Allow your relationships to shift into a new style of relating, and trust they will become what you need them to be. As you grow there will be relationships you need to review: do you want to continue investing so much into a particular relationship? If you are feeling immense pressure to stay pigeonholed for the sake of another's comfort and security, be wise and consult your Intuitive Self for the directives to take. Some people who do not align with your values and beliefs can be difficult to be around whilst you grow and try to move forward. If they are still stuck in their ways, you may need some space from them whilst you become clearer about your direction, and release the old thought patterns which no longer serve you. Let go of them temporarily, if need be, until you are more confident on your new path.

5. Honour others not on your path

Being unique in this world should be your first priority. Honouring others on their journey is a blessing, as it releases you from having to provide their needs, which may be very similar, or different, to your needs. Appreciating your differences will show you the value of their attributes, which may compliment yours. Just because you don't have their qualities, doesn't mean you cannot learn from those qualities. Allow them to teach you their positive attributes.

6. Find like-minded people

When you want to move forward, find someone to model how you would like to become, or does what you would like to learn. When modelling the behaviours and actions of another you learn how they think and feel, which makes the growing easier. You have a living testimonial of what you want to become, and you simply copy it. The saying "fake it till you make it" has much validity in this instance —

Self-Care

as you do, so shall you become. When you repeatedly do something new, those new thoughts are stored into your unconscious mind. Eventually you will not be faking it; when it is repeated enough you become what you are focusing on. Don't restrict yourself to one role model, have as many as you like. Look for people who have motivated or inspired you, not only celebrities and leaders, but family members and friends too. You'll be constantly surrounded by people with positive attributes. Keep a keen eye out, and don't be afraid to ask for help, or understanding. Most people are happy to talk about their positive attributes, and to help others gain life experience, as they have learnt to embrace their learning.

7. Purge

A feeling of clarity, and clearing, occurs as you purge old stuff from your personal and professional environments. Go through your environment and clean out anything you no longer use. Throw away anything you hang onto for old time's sake, unless you have a mighty good purpose for it in the near future, or seeing it reminds you of something special. Clearing out is incredibly cleansing, as you off load you move forward. When you release old stuff, new stuff arrives, it is universal law. You make room for the law of attraction to occur. So out with the old and in with the new.

8. Be true and self-serving

Be completely honest with yourself, and put yourself first. Being self-serving, and true to yourself, has absolutely nothing to do with selfishness. Selfishness operates from the ego mind, and occurs when you do not consider another at all, due to fear. Being self-serving is taking care of your own needs from the Intuitive Self, with the consideration of others, but honouring yourself first. Listen to how you feel, and allow yourself to take first place when it comes to needs being met, as this will help you stop expecting others to meet your needs. When you are true, and self-serving, you will notice you start feeling better about yourself. You may upset others because they want you to serve their needs before your own. However, remain true to your needs, or negotiate for a win-win between your Parent and Child if you feel pressure from others to do something against your inner guidance.

9. Reward yourself

Rewarding yourself has nothing to do with booking a holiday, updating your car, or fleeing to the closest shopping mall. Rewarding yourself is like patting yourself on the back, and acknowledging your efforts to grow by moving outside of comfort zones to conquer any fears. Have gratitude for the change you have brought into your life by taking yourself to your favourite place, or gathering with your favourite people, to enjoy life. These rewards can be as simple as a slow walk on the beach, a bush walk, listening to your favourite music, a massage, or some form of time out. Buying some reward may appear to be the first choice, but that feeds the ego mind, rather than the inner self. Choose loving rewarding things for yourself which will rejuvenate you, and your sense of self.

Self-Care

10. Mindfulness

Learning how to be present in your conscious mind is one of the major skills needed to be able to Observe, Analyse, and Act to move yourself in the direction you wish to be. Without mindfulness you can be caught up in inner conflict, feeling stuck, or unhappy. With mindfulness you have enough awareness to observe whether it is your Child or Parent driving your decisions. It tells you when you need to get some inner guidance from your Intuitive Self to get your Adult to put its hands on your steering wheel, and start driving your life in the direction it was meant to be going, which is one of purpose and passion, not unhappiness and despair. There are many ways to learn mindfulness. Meditation, yoga, tai chi, surfing, getting into nature, etc. all promote mindfulness.

11. Eat right and exercise

You will be guided in what you should eat by how you feel. Eat exactly what you feel you should eat. You know what foods are good for you and when you should eat, and if you don't, ask your Intuitive Self. We often ignore these signs and follow a clock for the times to eat, rather than following our natural body cycle as to when to refill our stomachs with good food. Stop being coerced by suggestive marketing and commercials that only benefit business. Many of those products have been created with a scientific approach to flavour, without regard for your health and well-being. When you pay attention to your body you will know what foods make you feel sick or ill after eating them. Smell your food. A great test for your food is that if you cannot eat and thoroughly enjoy a food when it is cold, then you probably shouldn't eat it. Fat, sugar and salt are masks to cover food that is not great fuel for your body. As I say, you have to put fuel in your vehicle for it to run at peak condition; if you put in oil and water as fuel, then expect rubbish results. The same goes for your body.

Your body will tell you when it needs exercise, and how much. When feeling sluggish, exercise is great to rekindle your sense of self and self-esteem. Follow your intuition again and do what your body needs. There is no competition with others in the 'body' world. You are uniquely different to any other person in the world. You only have one body and it is your temple. Accept your differences and love it.

12. Get into nature

Being around nature helps you feel more connected to your inner self. Nature will ground you. Being grounded is a sensation where you feel connected to Mother Nature, and the earth's wondrous gifts. I am sure you will have a preference as to what type of nature you enjoy most. Get some sunlight on your body or face, and enjoy the rays warming you. Walk into the water, as deep as you need, and feel the water embrace and cleanse your body. Dig your toes into the sand and feel the grains push beneath your toes. Allow the fresh breeze to stimulate your skin. Feel the bristles of the grass brush your feet or body, as you walk or lay on it. Touch the leaves of the trees, or hug them if you please. Think about how nature is perfectly in sync, and how you are also part of this perfection. The earth and its gifts are everywhere for you to enjoy. Take the time to bask in its

Self-Care

glory, and whilst you do that, become mindful. Give yourself thanks and appreciation for the time you have taken to enjoy nature.

13. Meditation and its benefits

Many people may try to meditate, only to quickly give up, because they become acutely aware of their inability to stop their run-away thoughts. They feel they will never achieve silence. I have been meditating for nearly thirty years, and it still takes me time to shut my thoughts down, especially when I have a lot going on, or my to do list is pages long.

Whilst the body needs repair from life's everyday stress, the ego mind leads us to believe it is serving us by ensuring we compete and compare ourselves to others, or their possessions, achievements, and reputations. The ego mind ensures our separateness from the oneness of the universe, and all the energy it contains. Meditation essentially tames the ego mind by allowing quite space, teaching us to listen to the ego mind without judgment, or the need to follow its orders or mind chatter. It will help to give you a sense of empowerment by seeing your inner self as separate from the ego mind. Taming the ego mind with meditation allows us to become more mindful and centred, with a focus on the Intuitive Self and your connection with the universal energy and Mother Nature. When our ego mind is overactive, the constant thoughts keep us from silence. This silence is where the re-connection can begin. With meditation practice, this silence comes, even if at first only momentarily, and the ego mind is quietened. You can then allow your thoughts to float by, and not be controlled by your ego mind.

Mind Chatter That Matters

With meditation, the gap between your thoughts is broadened, and a sense of connection to your true inner self is awakened. Meditation can then give you the ability to decipher the constant chatting, to listen, and become aware of the Intuitive Self voice so that you can follow it. It is then you can begin to feel more centred, and controlled, within your own environment. With this further understanding of your ego mind's thoughts, you will automatically create a more structured sense of self, as you can sense you are not just your thoughts, or body, or feelings.

Together with relaxation, and calming of the ego mind, meditation promotes the natural healing of the body, increased positive emotional states, and improved immune functions. Meditation promotes overall wellness and may help conditions such as[6,7]: allergies, anxiety, stress, arthritis, asthma, cancer, chronic pain and associated physical or emotional symptoms, depression, insomnia, high blood pressure, heart disease, and mood and self-esteem problems. There have also been sporadic studies showing that meditation, with forgiveness, helps to create a measurable improvement in pro-social, positive emotional skills. [8]

The technology now exists to analyse the brain's activity, and verify healing within the body as a result of the practice of meditation. The future is grand. All around the world more and more research is being conducted on meditation, specifically studying whether meditation has a significant effect in reducing the activity of the sympathetic nervous system, and increasing the activity of the parasympathetic nervous system. These sophisticated tools are being used in noting the effects of meditation, which include reducing the "fight, flight or freeze" response, and increasing the "rest and digest" response. The

Self-Care

research is looking at what goes on in the brain and in the rest of the body during meditation, and the impact of this on diseases and other conditions where meditation might be useful.[7]

Western traditional medicine now incorporates meditation and recognises the huge benefits it can provide. Western culture also now sometimes utilises Complementary and Alternative medicine in preference to drug therapy. Therefore people from western civilisations have both these resources to heal the mind and body, depending on individual needs and professional recommendations.

I believe meditation has helped me, and many others, to overcome difficulties in life and, considering its proven benefits, I think everyone should learn this skill. Persist with the practice, even if your thoughts don't seem to stop. You will eventually find a gap in your thoughts were you recognise a stillness, even if only for a few seconds at first. Just thank your thoughts for showing up, observe them, and let them go. You will find some free beginner meditation exercises on my website to download for your use. Enjoy.

14. Self-esteem and self-worth building

You may feel your self-esteem and self-worth never seemed solid and unwavering throughout your life. As you begin self-care directed by your Intuitive Self, you will feel your self-esteem and self-worth growing. This is how you rebuild and replace your sense of self into positive experiences, replacing the negative experiences and storage of the unconscious mind. Be patient with your sense of self, as it needs to grow into the new you.

15. Giving back

When you start to take better care of you, you will naturally want to give to others. In particular, when you have grown, and can see someone else struggling with their life, you will feel a tendency to guide, or offer some assistance to help make their life better. Make sure you are not imposing on them, instead help them find their own Intuitive Self's instructions. If you give to receive, you are driven by the ego mind. Giving without expectation will bring you more self-esteem and self-worth. Continuously check in with yourself to make sure you are not giving to receive. Giving to the community you live within is a great start. Contact your local government, and find out how you can volunteer, or look for charities near you. When you give to others you allow the Law of Attraction to work for you. Often what is returned to you is ten-fold, and from other sources.

16. Live your true passions

When you begin to follow the guidance of your Intuitive Self you will start to find your life purpose and passions, or will move further towards them. A passion or purpose could be anything from learning to paint, to becoming a global change maker, to moving towards helping the world's inhabitants, animals, or the environment. Follow the guidance you sense, and start making steps towards your true purpose and passion. Happiness will reign in your life, as you carve out your new life path doing what you love. Just remember it takes time to make some changes, but set your goals and get started on them, one step at a time. Often living your true purpose and passion has nothing to do with making money, or achieving material wealth,

Self-Care

but will bring it. So stay connected to the reason, rather than the material result!

17. Trust again

When we get hurt, or experience negative events, we tend to judge the world, or people, as untrustworthy. You may be in so much fear of being hurt again that trusting again seems an impossible task. Finding a new partner, after being terribly hurt by a previous one, can be daunting, but why impart your distrust on another who may deserve trust? But how do we learn to trust again, when we need to take time to see if trust can be given? When you begin to follow your Intuitive Self's instructions, you will learn to trust again. Follow your Intuitive Self, as your guidance system on what to trust, or not. Do you feel safe, or not? When something doesn't feels right (and you have not justified it in your ego mind), or if the red flags or bells are ringing, follow your gut feeling. It will not let you down. Observe, and analyse, and act! You will start to pay attention to it very quickly, to avoid leaving yourself in a situation where you will have your trust broken. It is when we are aware, but we ignore the warnings of the imminent betrayal in some manner, that we feel trust is shattered. Heed the warning signs, and you may prevent the trust being shattered. Take steps to self-protect, even against other fears you may be feeling. As you learn to trust your inner guidance, your decisions will follow. Trust will begin to infiltrate your views of the world, and people, as you replace any distrust you have stored into your unconscious.

Mind Chatter That Matters

18. Inner trust that you'll survive anything

When you learn to follow your Intuitive Self's guidance, know you can survive anything, as the inner support system grows to show you the gift of your learning. In every hardship of your life, there is often something which was ignored, or you didn't pay attention to. This is your lesson on what happens when the ego mind has overruled the Intuitive Self's guidance. When life's painful events occur, your Intuitive Self will speak quietly, clearly, and will be comforting. It will tell you everything will be all right. You will make it through. There will be another to love you. They are safe in heaven, and at peace. You just have to get through this day, and tomorrow will be better. This is held up for a reason beyond your understanding. We all have this voice, and you need to pay attention to its messages of love, and comfort. You will survive everything, so much better and more easily. Life becomes more balanced, happy and positive as you follow this guidance.

19. Respond with knowingness

Trusting in the messages and guidance shown to you will give you knowingness. You will start to understand how the phone rings, and know who it is. Or you will contact someone when they are thinking of you. This knowingness is your Intuitive Self. Pay attention to how often you just know things, and acknowledge the messages passed through to your ego mind. The ego mind will be surprised every time these events occur. However, you will learn to see how reliable the Intuitive Self's voice is. Pay attention, and give thanks for the upcoming information.

Self-Care

20. Be kind and give thanks

Have an attitude of gratitude, and you will shine from the inside out. Showing kindness to others, without expecting anything in return, will bring you much more inner happiness. Give thanks for the people and things which bring pleasure, assistance, or love into your life.

21. Take the road to true happiness and well-being

Know that following your Intuitive Self's guidance will take you on a road of true happiness and well-being. You will begin to take special care of yourself and put yourself in the centre of the picture of your life. You will no longer need to serve others to receive security or love, and therefore will increase your inner security, and self-love. Making decisions to put yourself at the top of your list will grow your self-esteem and self-worth. This true happiness is not motivated by the need to gain anything, but to honour you.

Mind Chatter That Matters

22. Forgive and see the good in everyone

Everyone has a dark and light side. It is sometimes difficult to see someone's good side if they have hurt or disrespected you in some manner. Forgiveness is imperative if you are to release your need to still be attached to them in a negative way. Understanding, and accepting that someone does not have the capacity to meet your needs, will give you the perspective you need to release your expectations of them, and this will allow you to forgive their inability to love and support you. This in turn allows you to forgive and release them. Forgiving someone who has hurt you is a loving act towards yourself, and releases you from the negative emotions you have held.

Practice changes for the next 30 days

Take the next 30 days to do something different in order to practice moving forward:
- Take a walk amongst Mother Nature's gifts
- Become mindful
- Pay attention to your Child voice today
- Pay attention to your Parent voice today
- Release the need to be perfect in anyone's eyes
- Be more present in the things you do
- Practice meditation
- Accept you are unique and different to anyone else
- Have gratitude for your life lessons
- Be kind to yourself
- Give thanks for those in your life

Self-Care

- Reward yourself with something immaterial
- Release the need to judge yourself
- Become aware of how critical you are about yourself
- Be kind to others
- Release the need to judge others
- Give back to others
- Respond with knowingness
- Feel free to make mistakes and try again
- Be flexible and flowing
- Let go of someone not on your path
- Trust your Intuitive Self voice
- Clear out unneeded material items
- Honour other people's journeys on their own paths
- Learn from a positive role model
- Trust someone you don't know much about
- Take a step towards your life purpose or passions
- Write a list of all your attributes and assets
- Look for the spark of good in someone
- Give thanks for your new growth and for your shift in awareness over the last 30 days, and repeat.

No matter how your journey transpires, how long it takes, or who is involved in your growth, be aware that people and things come into your life for a reason — learning and loving. Maybe they'll come for a season, maybe for a lifetime. Punishing yourself for your mistakes is not helpful to your growth; accepting that mistakes are inevitable for your growth will make your journey a much less bumpy ride. After all, you are here to live your life to its fullest.

Many blessings for having the courage to grow and find the home

Mind Chatter That Matters

within you!

Mind Chatter That Matters

Mind Chatter That Matters

REFERENCES

1. Locke, John. "An Essay Concerning Human Understanding (Chapter XXVII)". Australia: University of Adelaide. Retrieved August 20, 2010.
2. "Science & Technology: consciousness". Encyclopaedia Britannica. Retrieved August 20, 2010.
3. Sigmund Freud, New Introductory Lectures on Psychoanalysis [1933] (Penguin Freud Library 2) pp. 105-6
4. Freud, On Metapsychology (Penguin Freud Library 11) p. 89-90
5. https://www.lifeline.org.au/About-Lifeline/Media-Centre/Suicide-Statistics-in-Australia/Suicide-Statistics
6. Monahan P, Viereck EG, Meditation, the Complete Guide. Benenate B, Cone C editors. What is meditating? Canada: New World Library; 1999. p. xviii-xxi
7. National Center for Complementary and Alternative Medicine. Meditation for health Purposes (publication no. D308, page on the internet). National Center for Complementary and Alternative Medicine Web site. 2006. [cited 2007 Jul 27] Available from: http://nccam.nih.gov/health/backgrounds/mindbody.htm
8. Luskin F. Transformatic practices for integrating mind-body-spirit. Journal of Alternative and Complementary Medicine. 2005; 10(suppl. 1): S15-S23. Available from: http:www.ncbi.nlm.nih.gov/sites/entrez?cmb=Retrieve&db=pubmed&dopt=AbstractPlus&list_uids=15630819&query_hl=9&tool=pubmed_docsum

Mind Chatter That Matters

FURTHER INFORMATION

Liz Atherton is a Life Coach & Medium specialising in assisting people to uncover and release their unhelpful belief systems and blocks.

Finding the balance in life can be difficult with change imminent. Whether you are seeking a relationship, financial wealth, or success with a business or personal goal, Liz can help you find your own directives from your Intuitive Self.

Liz's goal in life is to help as many people as possible find true joy and understanding of the purpose and passions of their lives, and to

Mind Chatter That Matters

start living them!

Liz works with clients worldwide and you can on her website **lizatherton.com**, and on most social platforms.

Mind Chatter That Matters

AUTHORS NOTE

Like all of us, I have lived with lots of mind chatter. Ideas and opinions which often oppose each other. The rational part of my thinking would often overrule the other emotions, and gut instinct, and then I would experience the repercussions. Sometimes the hurt, and my disappointment in my own self and in other people, would result in confusion about which thoughts I should follow.

However, when it comes to creating a future we want, or making choices or changes in our lives, there is no exact science. Our thoughts are left to meander through the woods, trying to establish what we logically or strategically think is the correct course to take, whilst battling those senses which don't feel aligned with our logical thoughts. Most of us choose what seems logical, because we try to apply an exact mathematical science approach of cause and effect, to the possible outcome. If I do this… that will occur, if I do that… this will occur. But how many times do we get it wrong, to then go on and doubt our logical thinking?

When I was about eight years old, my father spoke about his own near death experience. Fifteen years later, my Dad was diagnosed with terminal cancer. I asked my father how he felt about dying, and he said he wasn't worried at all, because of his experience of absolute peace and love in the spirit world. I asked him to let me know when he was in the spirit world. Three days after his death I was to be freaked out with visions, and smelling him in my home. I knew it was real. The bittersweet tears rolled down my face, in the knowledge that life continues on in spirit, while those of us in bodies are faced with the humanness of materialism and limited perception.

My journey had begun. My grief was eased. The knowledge that death is a part of life, and that life is more than what we see materialistically, came alive in my mind.

My quest for finding my true nature began with a lot of dishevelment, and lessons, as I had no idea how to proceed.

I recall going to see a psychic medium, and my father came through to me in spirit, to announce I was going to do the work she was doing. I was scared to death, so to speak, but deep inside I knew she was right. I didn't know how I knew that, but I really, really knew

Mind Chatter That Matters

it. Fear kicked in, and shut the little voice down real quick! So I ignored her message, and got on with my life. After all I was only 25!

I would talk to my dad in spirit, and to God, and pray for comfort and healing even though I had no real concept of what God, or spirit, really was.

I began to meditate, and read new age and self-help books to find myself. Many months later I began to have strange experiences, which I didn't fully understand, during the meditation sessions. As the months went by I would see different movies or images flash before my mind, like I was in dream state. I would have gut instincts on what people were going to talk about, or what had happened in their lives. I would regularly finish people sentences. I'd have pictures flash in front of my mind, revealing where lost items were, when people were looking things. I thought it was everybody's experience, so I never really discussed it with anyone else, until I decided to do a psychic development course, and was told I was a "full blown medium".

I was gifted with one of the most loving souls on earth, my mother. She was a best friend who taught me love, compassion, empathy, and personal strength, qualities I was yet to experience in another soul. Mum passed away when I was 32. So my journey of grief began again, and along with the pain came further advances in my personal spiritual development.

I thoroughly enjoyed using my logical brain, but it seemed so far apart from my spiritual world. During my early years I felt my logical awareness and spiritual awareness were two separate parts of

Mind Chatter That Matters

me. They seemed to oppose each other, until I learned how to bridge the gap, and listen to the Mind Chatter That does in fact Matter!

I believe we can all listen to our own gut instinct, or Intuitive Self, to use our own inbuilt guidance system. If we have the right tools our logical minds and spiritual awareness can work together, rather than being worlds apart.

During the course of my life I have been shown how the mind works in conjunction with our Intuitive Self, and have been educated in this area too. This book has allowed me to share these wonderful understandings with you.

ACKNOWLEDGEMENTS

Producing a book of this nature requires the concerted efforts of many who have helped, and guided me along the way.

To my two beautiful miracles, my children Katie and Lachlan who doctors believed you would never arrive...however God had other plans! Individually you arrived into my life in perfect timing for my growth, love and life. Each of you have allowed me the space to be the best mother in the world with your relentless unconditional love for me that I have cherished like no other! You have embraced my gifts and loved me in a way that I cannot express how much you have contributed to my life. Your acceptance of my gifts and your support has encouraged me to follow my life path which I needed to take for my personal life journey. You are my sunshine, my light, my rewards, and my blessings, for all the effort, and love I spent on you. You are both worth every drop of your essence.

To my Mum and Dad, who live in spirit, and help me do my job the best way I can. I truly treasure you both.

To my editor Rocky Hudson for your perfection in English and grammar.

To my illustrators, for your tireless efforts of revisions, Marvel Banot, who designed my book cover, and Elvira Mikhralieva, for the interior images.

To Noel Campbell, my philosophical mentor for more than 20 years and my surrogate mother Auntie Mavis who loves me like one of her own. Both of your endless pursuit to help, love and inspire others, is unbelievable, and unwavering.

And finally to my guides who are also my teachers and confidants, I love you with all I am, and am meant to be to serve you and humanity.

Mind Chatter That Matters

Mind Chatter That Matters

www.ingramcontent.com/pod-product-compliance
Lightning Source LLC
Chambersburg PA
CBHW050538300426
44113CB00012B/2161